PLOUGHS

Winter 1999–00 · Vol. 25, No. 4

GUEST EDITORS
Madison Smartt Bell & Elizabeth Spires

EDITOR
Don Lee

POETRY EDITOR
David Daniel

ASSISTANT EDITOR
Gregg Rosenblum

ASSOCIATE FICTION EDITOR	ASSOCIATE POETRY EDITOR
Maryanne O'Hara	**Susan Conley**
FOUNDING EDITOR	FOUNDING PUBLISHER
DeWitt Henry	**Peter O'Malley**

ADVISORY EDITORS

Russell Banks	Stratis Haviaras	Robert Pinsky
Charles Baxter	DeWitt Henry	James Randall
Ann Beattie	Jane Hirshfield	Alberto Ríos
Anne Bernays	Fanny Howe	Lloyd Schwartz
Frank Bidart	Marie Howe	Jane Shore
Robert Boswell	Justin Kaplan	Charles Simic
Rosellen Brown	Bill Knott	Gary Soto
James Carroll	Yusef Komunyakaa	Maura Stanton
Madeline DeFrees	Maxine Kumin	Gerald Stern
Mark Doty	Philip Levine	Mark Strand
Rita Dove	Thomas Lux	Christopher Tilghman
Stuart Dybek	Gail Mazur	Richard Tillinghast
Carolyn Forché	James Alan McPherson	Chase Twichell
Richard Ford	Leonard Michaels	Fred Viebahn
George Garrett	Sue Miller	Ellen Bryant Voigt
Lorrie Goldensohn	Lorrie Moore	Dan Wakefield
Mary Gordon	Jay Neugeboren	Derek Walcott
David Gullette	Howard Norman	James Welch
Marilyn Hacker	Tim O'Brien	Alan Williamson
Donald Hall	Joyce Peseroff	Tobias Wolff
Paul Hannigan	Jayne Anne Phillips	Al Young

PLOUGHSHARES, a journal of new writing, is guest-edited serially by prominent writers who explore different and personal visions, aesthetics, and literary circles. PLOUGHSHARES is published in April, August, and December at Emerson College, 100 Beacon Street, Boston, MA 02116-1596. Telephone: (617) 824-8753. Web address: www.emerson.edu/ploughshares.

ASSISTANT FICTION EDITOR: Nicole Hein. EDITORIAL ASSISTANTS: Hannah Bottomy, Michael Homler, Kat Steiger, and Jean Hopkinson.

POETRY READERS: Tracy Gavel, Christopher Hennessy, Aaron Smith, Michael Carter, Jennifer Thurber, January Gill, Brian Scales, Renee Rooks, Michelle Ryan, Tom Laughlin, and Joanne Diaz. FICTION READERS: Darla Bruno, Elizabeth Pease, Laurel Santini, Eson Kim, Wendy Wunder, Kathleen Stolle, Amy Shellenberger, Nicole Vollrath, Emily Doherty, Kris Fikkan, Joseph Connolly, Debra DeFord, Billie Lydia Porter, Michael Rainho, Karen Wise, and Tammy Zambo.

SUBSCRIPTIONS (ISSN 0048-4474): $21 for one year (3 issues), $40 for two years (6 issues); $24 a year for institutions. Add $5 a year for international.

UPCOMING: Spring 2000, a poetry and fiction issue edited by Paul Muldoon, will appear in April 2000. Fall 2000, a fiction issue edited by Gish Jen, will appear in August 2000. Winter 2000–01, a fiction and poetry issue edited by Sherman Alexie, will appear in December 2000.

SUBMISSIONS: Reading period is from August 1 to March 31 (postmark dates). Please see page 233 for a description of the guest editor policy and for detailed submission policies.

Back-issue, classroom-adoption, and bulk orders may be placed directly through PLOUGHSHARES. Microfilms of back issues may be obtained from University Microfilms. PLOUGHSHARES is also available as CD-ROM and full-text products from EBSCO, H.W. Wilson, Information Access, and UMI. Indexed in M.L.A. Bibliography, American Humanities Index, Index of American Periodical Verse, Book Review Index. Self-index through Volume 6 available from the publisher; annual supplements appear in the fourth number of each subsequent volume. The views and opinions expressed in this journal are solely those of the authors. All rights for individual works revert to the authors upon publication.

PLOUGHSHARES receives support from the Lila Wallace–Reader's Digest Fund, the Lannan Foundation, the National Endowment for the Arts, and the Massachusetts Cultural Council.

Retail distribution by Bernhard DeBoer (Nutley, NJ), Ingram Periodicals (La Vergne, TN), and Koen Book Distributors (Moorestown, NJ). Printed in the U.S.A. on recycled paper by Edwards Brothers.

© 1999 by Emerson College   ISBN 0-933277-27-X

CONTENTS

Winter 1999–00

Cover painting:
Strong Winds by Kate Borowske
Oil on canvas, 18″ x 30″, 1998

Ploughshares
Patrons

This nonprofit publication would not be possible without the support of our readers and the generosity of the following individuals and organizations. An additional list of donor acknowledgements may be found on p. 235.

COUNCIL
Denise and Mel Cohen
Eugenia Gladstone Vogel
Marillyn Zacharis

PATRONS
Anonymous
William H. Berman / Houghton Mifflin
Jacqueline Liebergott
Estate of Charles T. Robb
Turow Foundation

FRIENDS
Anonymous
Johanna Cinader
In Memory of Larry Levis

ORGANIZATIONS
Emerson College
Lannan Foundation
Lila Wallace–Reader's Digest Fund
Massachusetts Cultural Council
National Endowment for the Arts

COUNCIL: $3,000 for two lifetime subscriptions and acknowledgement in the journal for three years.
PATRON: $1,000 for a lifetime subscription and acknowledgement in the journal for two years.
FRIEND: $500 for a lifetime subscription and acknowledgement in the journal for one year.
All donations are tax-deductible.
Ploughshares, Emerson College,
100 Beacon St., Boston, MA 02116

Introduction to the Fiction

The old year's over. So, too, the old century, the old millennium. Two thousand years of Western Civ! . . . Finished, achieved, collapsed.

Silly, of course, but it's how people think. Some people (oh, definitely a smaller set) are wondering whether the shiny new millennium which has just begun will have much literary fiction in it.

What does the future hold for us, producers and consumers of literary fiction? It's beginning to look like there will be more of the former than of the latter. Maybe there already are. The last ten years have witnessed drastic diminishment of the incredible shrinking trade publishing industry, which seems to have less and less room for variety in fiction, less room for any fiction at all. Meanwhile the embattled predicament of independent bookstores bodes very ill for "midlist" writers and whatever readers they have. The homogenization of all culture, driven as always by the dull and dreary demon of television, but reinforced on many other fronts, is a threat which continues to grow. That stale wind sweeps everything before it, and so a good many old-fashioned literary types (writers or readers) have come to identify themselves with the last withered leaf clinging (tenaciously, desperately, hopelessly . . .) to the windswept tree.

On the other hand, some unexpectedly positive things have happened, too. Hypertext fiction, enthusiastically predicted to supersede, in the Darwinian manner, its page-bound predecessor, has not done so. Hypertext has instead turned out to be a mostly different art form, interesting in its own right but with little at all to do with the literary fiction from which it sprang. The Internet, which certainly remains the world's largest vanity press, has also evolved into a surprisingly efficient and successful way of selling books in less than blockbusting quantities, and so looks likely to become a reasonable refuge for midlist writers and eclectic readers, too. Best of all, the book itself, this package of bound pages you now hold in your hand, maintains itself as superior technology for reading—superior to any computerized gadget likely to be invented.

But still, more producers than consumers, more writers than readers... to the point that a typical literary quarterly is apt to have more submissions than subscriptions. How did we wind up in such a fix? The short-term answer is obvious enough. In the 1950's, the idea of the writing workshop had barely cracked its eggshell, but now there are over two hundred such programs in the United States, and if we suppose that each of them annually turns out ten highly trained, highly qualified, degree-certified fiction writers, that's two thousand a year, and in ten years, twenty thousand... If all those people bought my book, I'd be set!... But they don't. They are busy trying to publish and sell their own books.

Talk about preaching to the choir. Even the choir won't listen. The singers are unruly, jostling each other, each of them eager for the rest to shut up, already, so that he or she can solo.

But there is a deeper cause, rooted in the American character, such as it is. In its laws, its culture, its ideology, and its "values," the United States has from its beginnings been inclined to set the individual above all. Life, liberty, and the pursuit of happiness are rights. Self-actualization and self-expression are rights.

Now, because the American ego is very strong, the individual American writer almost always intends, at the beginning of whatever text, to write a masterpiece. English and European writers (at least some of them) are apt to take a more modest journeyman's approach to the making of literary objects, but the American writer will always be trying for large importance, the Big Book, the Big Story. This consistently high level of ambition leads to ruin often enough, particularly when unaccompanied by talent or anything of interest to say, but it is a large and powerful engine for a national literature all the same. That engine has in fact made American literature the most vital and dynamic in the world, for the duration of the American Century... you know, the one that just ended.

Where that takes us is where we are now: a cacophony of everyone talking and nobody listening, everyone writing and nobody reading. Anarchy. It can't go on forever that way. Sooner or later it is bound to collapse on itself, a big, dark, bottomless sinkhole. Meanwhile, I rather like being an anarchist. It makes life less tiresomely predictable. There will be surprises, agreeable or not.

George Garrett, the old fox, once told me, re the literary scene, "The more pluralism there is, the better it is for everybody." It's true. And in spite of all those homogenizing forces there is a lot of pluralism, a lot of variety now.

For this issue of *Ploughshares,* I read my ration of dully competent short stories, degree-certified fiction, weary old workshop work. I also read more vital, arresting, unusual stories than the issue has room to print. Enough to suspect that there is a lot of germination going on down there where print hasn't seen it yet.

The shape of fiction to come has become a popular magazine agenda toward the close of the century—as presented in *Granta* a few years back, and more recently in *The New Yorker.* The collection of stories in this issue isn't meant to be anything like that. It is a cross-section of the best material that happened to come my way, but maybe as good a sample and indicator as any other such aggregate.

There are signs and signals of a culture in a period of anarchic upheaval. Men are writing in the voices of women; whites in voices of blacks—that sort of thing was quite recently against all the rules, but the rules are dissolving, and so much the better. We have in one story an episode of prescience and mental telepathy still more startling than the tornado of speed and violence in which it is set. We have the antique goddess Diana, manifested in the person of a crack addict. A couple of stories are downright surreal, while others catch and hold you just as hard by the insistent urgency of their voices. For my own part, I was captured by voice more than anything else, and especially by certain narrators who turn outward, bend the bars of the cage of rules which holds them in the text, peer out at us, demand that we look at them and listen to their tales.

That is the American way, that commanding egoism of the individual voice: Listen! Listen! Listen to me! For literary artists it is both strength and self-destructive weakness. But there is still enough strength in it to carry us into the third millennium, though exactly how far, or where, we cannot say.

The century's close is not, particularly, the end of anything. It would be silly to think so. Better to think that the year 2000 is just one more in the round of years. The last leaf has to let go in the end, but when it has, you can look for a greening. There'll always be one more way to tell a story.

ELIZABETH SPIRES

Introduction to the Poetry

The millennial moment. We can't know what it will mean, though we'll live through it and be lived by it. But with the new millennium in mind, we've chosen for our cover *Strong Winds*, a painting by the Minnesota artist Kate Borowske, seeing it as an emblem of the moment—the poet, or fiction writer, holding on for dear life in the face of disquieting change. A sixty-nine-year span separates the oldest and youngest writers in this issue: the eminent poet Josephine Jacobsen, 91, contributes two poems, and John McManus, 22, publishes his first story. In between are writers from every generation, scattered across the country, some recognizable "names," others starting out.

No one can know what direction serious literary activity will take in the twenty-first century, but I feel confident that—despite the quantities of mediocre, perfectly predictable poetry and fiction currently being written—an enormous amount of energy and talent is "out there" ready to propel American writing into the new millennium with a whoosh and a bang. Although we resisted the idea of limiting the work in this issue to a millennial theme, some of the poems here do speak for the times in topical and provocative ways: William Heyen's "Respects," Bruce Beasley's "Mutating Villanelle," Christine Stewart's "Spider Time," and Frank X. Gaspar's "The Lilies of the Field," to name just a few. No school or style is favored. Rather, I looked for poems that I thought were most successful on their own terms, rather than ones that mirrored a particular style or aesthetic. We hope readers find the offerings diverse, the voices individual and distinctive.

Last spring, in a poetry workshop that I was teaching in Baltimore, I asked my students to write about some aspect of the approaching millennium. The resulting poems ranged from the apocalyptic to the anticlimactic, a "bang" vs. a "whimper." I was especially struck by a sequence titled "The Year Gains Speed" by Samara Kanegis, too long to reprint here in its entirety, but I'll quote its concluding lines:

Time is running out.... We mark off the days,
work frantically toward those various turning points,
beyond which everything is invisible and huge.
This is the future: we can only travel at warp speed
toward the vast, hideous, gorgeous unknown.

Vast. Hideous. Gorgeous. The world we are living in *is* changing, the pulse of life increasingly impersonal, rapid, and isolated. It will be some years before we can put 1999 in any sort of context, literary or otherwise. But let this issue be a bridge between what was and will be, as we resolutely enter a new millennium.

JOSEPHINE JACOBSEN

A Blessing

I rejoice in the poems not written:
the cruelly discarded: the crippled,
the asthmatic, the anemic: the poem

about a photograph: about what love
is like: about how strangely I
felt that day: about something about me,

noticed. Bless you, go on the ash-heap,
that fine compost from muscle, blood, bone,
which fuels surely the green slick stalk.

written at MacDowell Colony, June 18th, 1983

Obit

The lovely lady posted in red
No Hunting. Last night
the supreme hunter crossed the meadow,
into the house, to the target.

Engaging Diane

A few things straight up: I'm mounting my stag, later I'll slash his throat, drain his blood; I'll gut him and he'll sate me, but for now he's my prop. My foot pressed firmly upon his bloody breast, his hoof in my hand, I speak.

My granddaddy was a Baptist minister, my daddy a newspaperman. I guess it runs in the family. Like them I'm going to tell you a story, with one caveat—this is my story; it has no moral, no intrinsic value; it's just a story about me. I remember, then relate past events. I will speak with authority. The implied conceit is that I will tell it like it was, that I am telling the truth. But I know better; you should, too.

I know that I've huffed machine cleaning fluid (Tywal), smoked angel dust, dropped acid, was stoned on pot every day for years, had a love affair with Quaaludes, snorted, shot, smoked cocaine—that's the hierarchy, right?—played with dope and drunk more than you would think possible to look at me. I'm slight, born under a cool sun. But I can hold my own. That matters or it may not. We shed brain cells like skin, synapses disappear, receptors abjure; we're shrinking, always shrinking, from the cradle. Believe nothing I tell you, or believe everything. Follow your temperament. You're not panning for gold, save yourself the trouble.

I admit that I'm unreliable. Every day I wake up hard, shaky and confused, yesterday irrevocably severed from today, tarnished by the night. In my bed, unconscious, I recast the day; I add and subtract. In the dark, I stalk myself, like the hunter the deer. Some flames burn brighter, others burn out. Perhaps, I'm shinier, brighter, more interesting than I might have been. A deluge of dime-store sentiment. Objectivity. It's all in your mind. How can the brain study itself? That's been a nagging question.

Last week I turned forty. That day, my birthday, I was heading downtown to my NA meeting, my home group; "Blast of Recovery" was the theme, something I could relate to, the "blast" part, anyway. I like to go downtown. My city is shaped like a wagon wheel, spinning; going nowhere except around; the center holds it together with its dead weight. This is my home, the forest of buildings, then the swath of the street.

I sat in the back of the bus next to the window, the metal of my knife cool against my shin. I pressed my face to the glass.

The man next to me wanted to sell me genuine gold chains, then crack. He touched my leg. I turned to look at him. He was wearing a wool cap, even though it was unseasonably hot. It was mustard yellow. The whites of his eyes weren't white. "Yo, check it out," he whispered, hand cupped around his mouth. He opened his bag, fingered the chains. I shook my head no.

"Yo, you ain't be no Five-O, right?"

I rolled my eyes.

"Cause, baby, I feel like I seen you before."

I kept my mouth in a flat line. "Today's my birthday," I said, rubbing my knife with my foot.

He squinted his eyes and made his decision. "Your birfday?" He slapped my arm. "Go, girl. Happy birfday! Well, you know, what else I got here be some good rock, too, baby. I got hold of some exclusive shit today." He palmed some glassine bags. His hand was rough and dry, his lifeline covered up. I felt my mouth water. "Tens, twenties... shit, for you, maybe I throw an extra ten in," he smiled, flashed a golden tooth.

A hit of crack is like a slow descent into a cool pond. You inhale, and sink, down. Everything recedes. You hold your breath tight and never want to exhale again. Your head kicks back, sometimes you hear bells ringing. There is no past, no future. Your brain is bathed in dopamine. The taste is something you never forget.

"Naw, man," I said. "I'm off the pipe." I hugged myself and shivered; then I turned away.

"Okay, okay, that's cool, that's cool. You all right," he said, palms up, crack repocketed.

I looked out the window, every line brightened by the rush of adrenaline, trying to swallow the taste. I looked through a dim reflection of myself on the glass, through my hungry face, my flat eyes. That's when I thought I saw him. The little hairs on my arms, legs, the back of my neck stood up. My nipples hardened. They say everyone has a double, so that must have been what I saw. I hadn't seen him in what, more than twenty-five years? And never in the light. I knew it couldn't really be him. Still. Still. The same mangy, curly brown hair down the back. The bone-skinny, stringy-muscled body in a too-tight faded T-shirt. Jeans slung around his hips; he had no ass, just a baggy spot where it should have been. Negative space. They called him Butt. His shoulders hunched, he was darting through the crowd. A cigarette hanging out of his mouth at an angle.

I jumped up as the bus screeched to a stop—so loud—and got off. Gravity fattened with the wave of heat at the door. Everything closed in; it was hard to breathe. This was a shitty part of town, an old neighborhood shopping district gone down. The smells of fried lake trout, rotting crab shells, fouled bodies, someone's sweet perfume, hung in the air. The sun bore down, faceless, unsmiling, unsympathetic. Its light was harsh; I'd forgotten my sunglasses. The trash lay dejected on the sidewalk.

I looked north up the street. He should have come sauntering along anytime, like someone slipping out of a R. Crumb comic. The bus exhaled its filthy breath and rumbled off. I waited and watched; I leaned against a streetlight, but he never showed. Was it a hallucination? A ghost? My higher power screwing with me again, juxtaposing Butt against the itch for the crack? Happy birfday. Right.

What was God's will? It popped like a punctured balloon. There was a package goods store right there! My feet walked right through the door. I bought one Ice Lite. My hands were shaking. Outside, I squatted in front of a cheap wig store: pageboys, falls, extensions. I squatted down against the wall to consider the crack, to consider Butt. The brown paper bag rustled as I uncapped the beer and let its cool clear water fall down my throat. One hit would be kinda nice. It being my day and all.

There was some disused land where all the bad kids and strays hung out. I don't know why it was there. It was overgrown with rhododendrons, azaleas, raspberries, yews, canopied with old oaks, tulip poplars, and pines. When my parents broke up and my mother moved my brother and me into the city from the country, I started slipping away from the confines of our tiny rowhouse, off the noisy block, out of my dense neighborhood, and playing there, because it felt more like home. I was thirteen and I often played with the knife my father had given me, showed me how to use. I made crude creatures out of roots and twigs. *"In the pines, in the pines, where the sun never shines..."* I played there at night, skulking at the edges, scouting.

There was a big circle of oaks where everyone congregated. At its center was a makeshift fire ring, littered with beer cans, cigarette butts, roaches, broken glass. There was a core group of seven or eight boys that hung there, but on a summer night there might be thirty or forty kids sitting around, drinking, getting high, faces lit unevenly by a fire if it wasn't too hot. I'd watch from the distance, from across a narrow creek, clear water singing, sipping my own beer, stolen from the neighbor's garage. They got used to me creeping around. "What's that noise?" one of them would ask.

"Oh, it's just that crazy little girl," a voice would return. "Or, maybe a dog..."

As the summer wore on I dared to slip in closer, near enough to hear. I liked to listen to their talk, whittle on a stick, and watch them. When the boys were alone they talked about all the girls they jumped, that and sports, and dope. They wrestled, rolling through the leaves, until one would give. Each took a turn as my imaginary boyfriend.

One night late, I was squatting next to a tree, trying to light a cigarette, when a twig next to me snapped. I froze up, my lighter cocked and burning. A hand touched my arm. I shrugged it off.

"Did I scare ya? I was just playing with ya." I recognized the voice. "Wanted to see if I could catch you." It was the one they called Butt. He was the skinny one with the thin face and the long hair and big hands. One of them lost itself in my hair. "You got soft hair," he whispered. "Hey, I saw ya on the street the other day. You were wearing green shorts and a halter-top. You looked so long and tall, your hair all hanging down. You're pretty sweet, you know that?"

I pulled back, my lighter dropped to the ground. "Get away from me," I said. "I've got a knife."

He laughed and dropped his hand. "I'm not gonna do nothing, little girl. Just wanted to tell you I liked your stuff."

Out on the sidewalk I finished my beer. The next bus stopped, but I didn't move. It was too late to make the meeting now, anyway. And I wanted another drink. Shit, it was my birthday. I was forty years old. If I wanted a drink, I would have one. I walked north up to 32nd Street, turned east. One of my bars was there.

"Well, we ain't seen you in a while, hon," Denise said. "What'll it be?"

"A beer and a shot," I replied. *Sally Jessy* was on the TV. It was around 11:30. Denise put the beer and shot down in front of me and went back to *Sally Jessy*. I lit a cigarette and let my thoughts drift. The place was empty except for old man Charlie. A cool, dark hole.

Butt began to seek me out. I moved around a lot. It got to be a game. He'd find me and sit with me. The others made no notice. We would talk, him about his crazy parents: they'd had five kids, then got sick of it. Decided they'd had enough. Decided they weren't Catholics anymore. Pulled their kids out of St. Anthony's. Joined an encounter group. Now there was a naked headless mannequin in the living room. And they dealt dope. I told him how my brother and me were twins but born on different days, how Mom never married Dad, how he was already married.

Butt brought me things: cigarettes, beer, joints. He got me high the first time. The sweet taste alone was intoxicating, the heavy smell of the smoke, the way it hung in the air. He would brush against me when lighting the joint, run his hand across my back.

One time he brought me some earrings: two little hearts, each run through with an arrow. "I lifted them from the Kaufmann's," he'd said.

"My ears aren't pierced," I'd said, sadly. I felt stupid.

"They aren't?" he'd asked, surprised.

"No."

"Mmmm," he sighed. "Hey, I think it's cool, your ears aren't pierced." He put his arm around my shoulder. He whispered in my ear, "Really cool." He brought his fingers to my lobe and rubbed it slowly. "Yeah..." Then he'd turned my face to his and kissed me.

I jumped up. "I gotta go now," I said and ran off. I went home and sat in my room, in the dark, playing it over and over in my head. I was excited. I was scared. I was a virgin.

Butt took his time. He didn't push me. He let me get used to him. His nearness. He didn't try to kiss me again for a long time. He saw that I was jumpy. But he had a way of ending up on me. Before I noticed, he'd have his leg on top of mine. Then I'd move and he'd never acknowledge it. His hand on my rib, his breath in my ear, his shoulder touching mine. He turned me on to speed— talk, talk, talk, talk. Then acid. He let me trust him. I trusted him. He began to talk about touching me. He told me that he wanted to touch me. He made me think that I wanted him to. When he said that I'd like "making love" with him, that it would feel good, I believed him.

"You want another one, hon?"

"What?" I asked, confused.

"You want another beer?" Denise asked.

"Oh, yeah, yeah, and another shot." *Sally Jessy* was over, now *Geraldo* was on. Old man Charlie waved at me from the other end of the bar. I waved back. I had to pee. I got up and went to the john. On my way back I stopped by the pay phone and called up Q.

"Hey, girl, where you been?" she asked. "I been missing you."

"I took a little vacation," I said. "So, can you help me out?"

"Shit yeah, I got some gooooood shit, girl, real good," she said. "Uh-huh."

"Okay, I'll be up in an hour or so," I said.

"An hour or so? You can't get up here no sooner?"

"Nope."

"Shit, you getting drunk, ain't you?"

"Yep," I said.

"I don't know how you can do that shit," Q returned. "It rots your gut. Later."

"Later." I hung up the phone and returned to my stool.

One night toward the end of that summer, while I was sitting against a tree, scraping my knife against a root, listening to the clear tinkle of the creek, Butt crept up and said, "I got us some good stuff tonight, girl."

"What?" I asked.

"Four-way windowpane," he replied.

"What's that?"

"Only the best acid money can buy. My dad turned me onto it." He squatted down in front of me. "Open your mouth. Lift your tongue." He held the back of my head. I felt a tiny piece of something like sharp plastic. "Keep your tongue down," Butt said. He'd brought some beer, too. The night was clear and cool, no clouds, the moon almost full. It lit up the woods. We sat and drank the beer, waiting to get off, listening to the sound of the wind rustle the dying leaves.

The stars brightened in the sky. "Hey, look," I said. "The stars are blinking off and on."

"You're starting to get off," he said, his hand stroking my hair, burrowing down into my neck. He kissed me, slipped in his tongue, slowly washing my teeth. My whole body was tingling. I felt like I couldn't breathe. His tongue was a gag. I broke the kiss, panting. "Wow," I said. I rubbed my thumb back and forth over the blade of my knife, which I still held. The skin caught and bled. I brought it to my mouth.

"Gonna let me jump you tonight, Diane?"

I couldn't speak. Butt considered my silence acquiescence. He pushed me back to the ground and moved over me.

I was really getting off. The wind picked up, gusting over and around us. I was frozen, unable to move. Butt was over me kissing my neck and face. His mouth found mine again and he pushed his tongue in. I heard drums beating in my ears. He pulled back and unbuttoned my shirt, unzipped my shorts. I felt like I was watching us from above. I couldn't act. Butt was suddenly hurried. He pulled my shorts and underpants down roughly. "Hey," I tried to say. Fear started to prickle. Then he pulled his own pants down. I'd never seen a penis before. Nothing to judge it against. But it seemed huge. It jutted out from his skinny body, shining. "No," I tried to say. "No."

"Spread your legs," he panted. "Spread your legs! Shit, I'll do it," he said when he got no response from me. He spread my legs and began to blindly stab at my groin.

My brain and body remarried. My body thawed. This knowledge overwhelmed me: I could not have that thing in me. I understood that I didn't want it there. I never had. I tried to wriggle out from under him. I couldn't get any words out. "Stop," I would have said. I could hear the creek water rushing past. The moon shone down from above. It bathed my hand, my knife. I saw it shine; then I used it. I brought it up under his ear. I had no hesitation. I sliced deeply. He groaned then collapsed on me. His warm wet blood rained down on me.

Dead weight is heavy. It was work to push him off. I was breathing shallowly, rapidly. I stumbled a few feet, knelt down against a tree. I wiped my blade clean. Then I vomited. Soon after I heard leaves rustling, things crashing through the trees. I stood up. I heard a low growl, then another. Two dogs stood on either side of Butt, eyeing each other, sniffing at his pants.

I ran, tripping over sticks and rocks. I ran away. I heard them start to snarl and growl louder. I didn't go back. I was so high. I went to the schoolyard near my house and lay in one of the tubes all night. I felt between my legs, searching for damage. I was wet down there. I brought my finger up and put it to my lips. Blood there as well.

Someone touched my arm. I started. "How you doing, gal?" old man Charlie said. "I ain't seen you in a while."

"Fine, fine, Charlie," I said. I patted the barstool while I stood up. "Sit down, Charlie. Lemme buy you one."

His pale old eyes lit up and his face cracked. "Thanks, dear."

I ordered Charlie one, paid Denise, and left. The heat again blanketed me at the door. I needed money. I walked back to Greenmount and hit the bank machine at the Nation's Bank. The bus rolled up as I finished my business. I got on and went on up to Winston Avenue. I got out at the Popeye's. Q liked chicken. She never ate. I bought her a few pieces. "Let's party," I said when she opened the door, handing her the chicken.

She hugged me to her thin body. "Yeah, girl." Q's hair was in a scarf; her eyes darted quickly around the room. "You got some cash?"

"Got four twenties," I told her.

"Okay, I be right back. Don't go nowhere," she grinned. "I'm so glad to see you."

* * *

A hit of crack subdues the beast. For a moment he's dead. You're like a lion after a big kill. You stare out of your eyes and process images. You're full and content. There is no thought. You bear no responsibility. That's the taste you never forget.

"Hi, my name is Diane and I'm an addict."
"Hey, Diane."

When I say "I," that's fiction. There is no absolute, no history. Other players might argue the account if they could, or cared to. Some may be in the grave, others in the bar; others still would be better off in either place. They are slumped on their couches, arms and legs, torsos rotting, waiting, simply waiting. For what? Rubbing sleep from their eyes, facing the days, the months, the years, with less and less. I grow more facile with time. That makes me an optimist, and a teller of tales.

Missing World

In the grand scheme of things,
These words are smaller
Than one pixel in a black
And white photograph,
A grain of sand, smaller
Than molecules—no—
Smaller than that.
Zoom out, as in those old
Science films in junior high,
From one letter of one
Of these words, out—
To the room, above
The house, the street, beyond
The neighborhood, up and out
To rows of roads,
Circles of cities,
Then vaguer and cloudier,
To swirls of white, green, and blue,
To the globe of the earth
And on, pulling backwards
To the fine minimal web of planets,
Still in reverse, slower now,
To the sparkling veins of star
Systems, the rich, billowing
Arms and legs of purple
And orange gas, twisting oddly
Like deep-sea creatures
Who never see the light,
Outwards still to the spirals and coils
And corkscrews of galaxies

Like amoebas hustling across
The cold emptiness of a glass slide.
Stop. Here words must
Overlook, exclude, deny.

Spider Time

I brush aside a spider from my arm,
but he returns to scale the mountain of my knee,
scuttle across my book, over page 64, and off the edge.
Disoriented, thwarted, he pauses in the grass,
then drops down, swaying from the tip of a green blade.
Swooping from one to the next, the afternoon light
picking out the sticky, wispy strands of his sturdy rope,
he spins his story, his web of evolution,
from an instinct built over millions of years.
And what of my own instinct?
It rolls over sleepily in the sun, its needs met,
survival's urgings supplanted by boredom,
a sort of wet nurse to us all.
No longer do we live in spider time—
the hidden knowledge that once directed us,
our gift of sentience, dull from disuse.
Will whoever comes after and catalogues our primitive bones,
discovers our crude but ambitious dwellings,
deciphers our writings, our *science,*
will they marvel at how long we lay pooled
in an evolutionary stasis of our own making—
one of public toilets, frozen foods, and the morning-after pill?
They will know what we did not;
they will ridicule our reasoning and argument for and against
those huge, dark instigators—Order and Chaos,
how we ignored the improbable coincidences and calculated
    miracles
reaching down through Nature's vast and random history,
through the web, connecting me to this spider,
poised there.
Tomorrow he may die,
the wind or rain destroy all traces of his work, but still
he will outlive me, in one form or another—
spin his web in other places,
proving and improving his species.

Of this I am certain: were Darwin here,
crumbs in his beard, coughing and drinking tea,
he'd not give me a second glance,
all the passion and poetry of his prose,
saved for the spider.

The Lilies of the Field

One of those early summer days, driving west on
Carson Street, heading for parts unknown, singing
aloud in my head, saying *Lord, Lord, what am I to do?*
Not a heaviness in my heart, not a lightness in my heart,
but the usual hum and rush of living in this city of bungalows
and smokestacks and barges and ocean. I was trying
to keep my promises, but I didn't know how—I wasn't
expecting a sign, exactly. I wasn't expecting the family
on the parkway strip, right there on Carson Street,
the old green pickup truck, and the blankets spread
in a row on the grass—and they were selling their things,
everything, from the look of it, the quick backward-rolling look
you get from a motoring car, the one way to see the world
at this hour in our century, the *elect* way because the dimension
of time doesn't allow you a single chance to delude yourself:
this is the universe expanding—shirts, pants, a child's
car seat, bright plastic things strewn like a rummage
sale, but right there on the parkway grass, the traffic
swooshing by, and that family—five, six of them, kids,
everyone, out on the grass selling things no one would
ever want to buy. You had to ask yourself, you had
to feel things: how did they come to this? All this
in an instant, in the passing shot, in the frame of
a car window. You had to consider how much of the
Sermon on the Mount was ambiguous. You had to
at least entertain the idea that the Buddha was clearer
in his communications. You had to marvel at the
enormous figure of the angel Gabriel giving shorthand
to Mohammed. I don't think that family spoke English well.
You could get a sense of that by the look of them. We've
all been there: you nod and smile and point, you pull out
a few words, they pull out a few words, there is a little
embarrassment, those small laughs that are accompanied

by a quick forward jerk of the head. It's how to get along.
You can buy a pair of shoes that way for a dollar and a half.
You can get a Webster's dictionary for fifty cents. You
can get a King James Bible for nothing if you don't mind
the inked inscription inside the front cover: *Presented to*
Bruce Stoltley by the North Long Beach Presbyterian Church,
September 29, 1958. I know that the dangerous thing is believing
that you love everyone, every suffering thing, even while
you know that you would tear out someone's lungs or step on
a person's heart in the right hour of the right day. How
the sun sits so high these days, so different from its low
pale winter path—how everything is exfoliated in the light,
how everything begs to mean something other than itself.
I am not talking about the problem of meaning only one thing,
but the truth about meaning all things, all at the same time.
Behold the lilies of the field, for instance. *Behold the birds.*
Behold the tattered colors of worldly possessions spread
out on the city green, their sudden speed, backward
in the side window of the automobile. How they vanish,
but never really vanish. How they persist. How *everything* toils.

Education by Stone

after Joao Cabral de Melo Neto

To go to it often, to catch its level impersonal voice,
says de Melo Neto in the graveyard's moon-white orchards.
To being hammered, the lesson in poetics, the speller of spells,
he says. What did you learn standing with the east wind cutting
over the fields of tilting stone, above the beloved dead, who
must love the stones in the field as they love the field?
As the stone loves, in turn, in its way, hardened and
    misunderstood:
It is not past loving. It is only past loving in one way of speaking.

So the stone teaches, and the stones teach, and you sat at their feet
and stumbled over your lessons. The stones made a catechism
for you, dense and like their hearts, resolute and singly knowing.
Who will recite like stone, like the stones? Who will bear
with compacted heart the inscriptions of the names of so much
that was beautiful? Will you? In their toppled kingdom, will you?

Mutating Villanelle

Because God wants us to have indefinite life, like Him,
Richard Seed intends to electroshock an egg
to implant his image and likeness into Gloria, his wife

    (to implant into Gloria, his menopausal wife, his
      shocked image and likeness)

after inducing quiescence in its nucleus (moon-pause)
so his DNA might nest there and live forever,
cloned, and cloned, indefinite life God wants us to have, like
    Him.

Enucleated oocyte, like the lamb-clone Dolly's.
Lamb of God, who takes away the sins of the world,
(implanted sin, aboriginal, in the image and likeness of God,
    Gloria

in excelsis Deo) . . . *Heaven forbid,*
I wouldn't trust him to breed a tadpole, his ex-wife said.
God wants us like Him, in His image, after His likeness, seed

    (having shed "indefinite"
      having shocked into fusion the two mutating
      refrains)

fallen on fertilized ground. Nucleus hollowed, egg
shocked into taking the alien
cell into its image and likeness, glorious implantation.

    (lamb-
    clone, 237
    grotesque miscarriages
    before it was born)

Lamb of God, you take away our imperfections,
through manipulation of the flawed genes.
Because God wants us to be like Him, indefinite
    (because God wants us,
    wants us clones of Him)
how soon will the womb of Gloria be implanted with the
    image and likeness of seed...

    (Enucleated
    iambs, perfectible
    refrains [to hold oneself
    back, forbear],
    imperfectible rhymes
    [glory/story, likeness/
    Loch Ness]:
    grotesque
    miscarriage
            indefinite
            likeness,
    glory, electroshock, tadpole, rough beast, seed)

how soon will the womb of Gloria be implanted (*Hail, O favored
    one, the Lord is with thee*) with the image and likeness
    (fore-born) of Seed...

Other People's Mothers

While Wanda had an abortion, I had lunch with her mother. "Please," Wanda had said, swathed in large paper napkins, "just get her away from here." Then she closed her eyes, and her boyfriend, Ramon, nodded, so I took Wanda's mother to a Chinese dumpling shop.

Once there, she told me the old story about how Wanda's father wanted to name her Espinaca. Spinach, in Spanish. How Wanda was a whiny child who never could decide on what flavor of ice cream to order. Once they had to leave the store without any ice cream at all.

She kept mispronouncing Wanda's boyfriend's name and dropping dumplings. Finally she stabbed a dumpling through the middle with one chopstick and used the other chopstick to saw it in half. "I just love other cultures," she said, "but this is ridiculous."

Wanda's mother: long, gray hair in a single braid, with cheekbones that shot her face forward into your business. Wearing a purple smock with orange trim and tapping her bitten fingernails on the table—"Do you think they're done? Oh my. Oh my shit."

I said, "It's going to be okay, Nancy," or some stupid thing. She stared at me.

"This is my granddaughter or grandson, theoretically. Although a fetus isn't yet a human being. And a woman has a right to choose. But someone's vacuuming out my daughter's insides. Since she came from my insides, et cetera, things aren't as separate as you think, missy. And let me tell you, if it had been legal in my time, I would have done the exact same thing with Wanda." Wanda's mother straightened her smock.

"So do you have regrets now? With Wanda?"

"There's always regret after you act, or don't act. That's true of any big decision."

She was so imperious with her garish clothes and outdated perfume, I said, "Will you be *my* mommy?" She laughed. Then she stopped laughing with a frown and put her hand on her stomach.

When I came back to the clinic, Wanda asked, "How is she?" She was hooking her bra and pulling her sweatshirt over her head.

"Fine," I said. "Stoically liberal."

"Where is she?"

"Getting sick in the bathroom."

We waited at the ladies' room door for Wanda's mother until she reemerged, smiling at Wanda with watery eyes and arms stretched out. "My baby," Wanda's mother said, then halted, knowing she had said the wrong thing.

Me, I lost my own mother, although she's still alive. Some nights in my apartment I light a fifty-cent glass candle with a picture of St. Jude painted on one side. I recite the prayer pasted on the back—Oración a San Judas Tadeo—knowing little Spanish, besides *espinaca* and some swear words. "*Glorioso apóstol, San Judas siervo fiel,*" I say, "bring my mother back to me," but the painted face says, There are other mothers.

I dated Macon for two years because his mother took my arm when I met her and said, "Make sure he eats broccoli, okay?"

For me, more than a mother. She was my second-chance mama. I loved her, hemmed my pants for her. I followed her around her apartment, asking questions: How do you knit? What are basted eggs?

Macon's mother prefaced her sentences with "Guess what?" She told guests that I was her third daughter, which caused confusion when Macon and I held hands and kissed.

I learned the rules—what to cook for holidays, what to say about the movies we saw together. If there was a dog in the movie, it was a good movie. If there were guns in the movie, it was a good movie.

Macon's mother thought I needed "toning down," so she gave me a book entitled *Wherever You Go, There You Are.*

"Buckaroo Banzai," I said.

"And likewise to you," she said. She spelled Chanukah wrong on the card, but I'd imagine that most Southern Baptists would.

"You run around too much. You need to *smell those roses.*" With each word, she pounded the cutting board with her sharp fist.

"It's hard to manage my time. A girl's got to make a living," I told her, dicing garlic.

"It's just as easy to fall in love with a rich man as it is to fall in love with a poor one. Marilyn Monroe said so, and look how well she turned out."

I stared.

She amended, "Well, before that overdose business. Anyway," pointing the turkey baster at me, "*you* need a rich one."

"But what about Macon?" I asked her. Her son. In the next room, his balding head shone in the lamplight. He pulled a hair out of his mouth, then looked at it.

"Oh," she said. "Well, there is that."

She called the day I broke up with Macon. I cried so hard, the phone kept slipping from my hand.

"I'm just so shocked," she said.

I mumbled something that had no words.

"Lunch," she promised. At her house. I'm still waiting to be fed.

When I was small, my mother told me the things that a mother tells little girls in order to get along. She told me that when you drink something hot, never sip it the first time. Instead, dip your top lip into the cup. That way it looks like you're drinking, but instead you're testing.

"What if you burn your lip?" I asked.

"It's not as bad as a tongue."

So I did, burned my lip with the milk-laced tea, it was too hot. I thought of what would hurt least—an elbow, an earlobe. Nowadays I poke my finger in the cup, even in restaurants, on dates.

My mother told me, "No, serial killers are not people who kill cereal. No, numbers have no smell. No, dead bugs don't dream."

She arranged concentric circles of bite-sized dabs of cream cheese in a pastel plastic bowl. I scooped them up with my fingers and poked them into my mouth. She picked my grapes off their spines. She pretended that my sandwich could talk, flapping its bready lips. "Eat me," it growled in her hands.

My mother sang "You Are My Sunshine," skipping over the part about waking up and finding your sunshine gone. She pulled warm clothes out of the dryer and dropped them on top of me at naptime.

She said, "There are 2.8 calories in each and every stamp."

She did mother things.

She told me that rivers come from rain.

Next was Frederick. His mother had grown up poor in the Depression. She often quizzed me:

"Do you ever leave the knife in the peanut butter jar and just close it up tight like this?" She screwed the top on. The knife clunked thickly inside. When I said, "No, never," she put the jar back on the shelf. "Saves," she said, nodding her head.

"Do you ever leave the cheese cutter in the bag with the cheese? Saves."

"Do you ever put the cooking pot in the refrigerator with the food still in it? Saves."

She told me about sewing across the toes of her old torn socks and putting them on her kids' feet so they'd be warm walking to school, with socks that ran all the way up their legs.

During her entire weeklong visit, she insisted on staying in our one-bedroom apartment. She said, "Oh, just throw me in the corner with a chocolate bar, and I'm happy as two clams." We gave her our bed and slept on the floor ourselves. In the morning she said that the mattress was a bit hard, which it was.

She said, "There are three ways of telling time: where you lived, where you worked, and whom you went out with. It's a good idea to keep these things written down on a piece of paper."

When I lived with Frederick, I loved him with a subtle desperation that was tied to anticipated loss. I watched my diet, eating whole grains. I washed everything twice. I put pennies in a jar, skimped on tips. When he finally did leave me, I felt dazed and relieved. As if my grip had grown so tight, only after it was broken could I again move my hands.

Frederick's mother didn't call me. She was on a singles' cruise at the time of the breakup, and she probably forgot after that point.

Frederick wrote his goodbye note on the back of our electric bill, which was in his name. I tore it up with the tips of my fingers and flushed it down the toilet, a silly smile on my face. "Saves," I said.

When I was about six, my mother had begun sleeping all the time.

She took a nap right after making my stepfather's tepid breakfast and sacking any lunches for the day. The kiss at the door, then she moved toward the couch as if she were walking down the middle of a canoe. Once outside, I watched her through the tinted front windows of the house. Every morning she fell backward onto the couch, picked up her book, laid it like a tent on her pink terrycloth chest, and closed her eyes. Then I ran off to the waiting bus at the bus stop.

My teacher showed us the parts of a peanut. She told the girls, You can be firemen, or mailmen. Or policemen. I thought about my stepfather's fists when my mother typed up her résumé, and my mother's bruised face the next morning.

After school I always rushed home to tell my mother all the new ways I had learned that she was wrong. She was usually awake when I came home, with her cheek creased from the seams of the upholstered couch pillow. She poured orange juice and pulled out the peanut butter jar. Then she left me an open-faced sandwich with the spoon still stuck in the middle as she went to lie down.

At night, after my stepfather hung up his pants and my mother toppled back to the sofa, I went upstairs to my room, there being no other place. Hoping my mother wouldn't wake up as my stepfather locked my bedroom door behind him, saying, "You like this"; as I said, "Okay."

When I finally told her, she kicked him out. After a couple of years.

"You ruined my marriage," she told me.

When my friend Wanda was eleven, she was walking down the street with her mother. Six or seven teenage boys started hooting from a fire escape railing. "Hey, baby, hey, mama," things like that. Wanda's mother stopped in the street, confused. Encouraged, the boys yelled more loudly and lewdly, and Wanda started tugging at her arm. "Come on, Mom!" She knew the boys from school. Finally, Wanda's mother put her hands on her hips, looked up, and shouted, "If you boys don't cut that out, I'm going to come up there and *rape* you." They shut up, abruptly. Wanda cried from embarrassment then, but when she tells the story now, she laughs so hard that she has to go to the bathroom.

* * *

I had been seeing Jake for a year when his mother announced her second visit. It was close to Mother's Day. After we hung up the phone with her, my left eyelid swelled up immediately. The first time I met her, I had gotten a rash all over my upper arms and inner thighs.

She pinched my shoulder when she saw me. "The weight looks good on you," she said. I wasn't aware that I had accumulated weight, and when we ate lunch together, I ordered a cheeseburger and thought, Fuck it.

That night Jake wanted to have sex, but I wondered if he was thinking about his mother, too. So we held hands as he slept and I didn't. With my other hand, I pinched the skin over my stomach and thought of that old commercial, "Can You Pinch an Inch?" I pinched many inches, then lay in bed with pinch-bruises tingling on my skin.

The next day, we picked up Jake's mother at her hotel. In the lobby she suggested that I take Jake's last name, "just in case." His last name is Holtzenweiser. Jake asked her, "Are you serious?" She tilted her head on her neck like an injured bird. "It was good enough for me," she said.

I had plucked some eyelashes out of my left eye in the attempt to reduce the swelling. I plucked a few too many. Jake's mother asked, "What happened, a kitchen fire?" She was sympathetic, so I said yes. Jake wrapped a strong arm around me and announced that he had bought twenty lottery tickets. "We've all got it made," he said.

Jake's mother checked out of her hotel the last night of her visit and stayed at our place. Making dinner, I pulled baked olives out of the hot oven. I forgot to put the mitts on first. I managed to deposit the sizzling glass pot safely on the stovetop before running to the freezer and grabbing the ice cube trays. Jake pulled at my hands and told me to let him see. They were white and already blistered.

Jake's mother wrapped them in clean dishrags and taped them shut with duct tape. This felt worse, then better. Jake fed me dinner with a fork. His mother pretended that this was ordinary.

Later, I heard them talking in the next room while I lay in bed. I couldn't hear their words, but I knew that they were talking about me from their voices. I did hear "poor thing," the one thing I was supposed to hear. I translated it into Spanish, then Japanese. *Pobrecita. Kawaiso.*

The day Jake's mother left, I watched him make sandwiches for her plane ride. He sliced havarti cheese, tomatoes, avocados, and then stuffed sprouts in the cracks. She packed her dirty socks into neat rolls.

She started to kiss me goodbye at the door, but I was beginning a bad cold and didn't want to infect her. My nose itched, and my eyes were watering. How much more of this can I take? I thought. We walked her outside.

"Bye, Mary Margaret," I said as she walked down the sidewalk to her rental car.

"Call me Mom," she said, and I waved. She wasn't my mother. My mother sent me Water Pik attachments for my birthday if she remembered, which she didn't that year. My mother said that I was her least favorite child, although I was her only child. My mother said, "Don't call me, I'll call you," and didn't.

When Jake's mother called, safely home, we said that I was fine now. We pretended that this was true.

However, eyelid swollen, hands wrapped in gauze, sneezing on the couch, I thought about how my body comes from somebody's body. This is what's true. Yet impossible.

A few months after he left, my stepfather came back for a few weeks. My mother stopped sleeping and spent a lot of time doing laundry. My stepfather called me Liar. "Hi, Liar. How was school today?" When I told him, "Fine," he said, "Sure it was."

One evening he made a lot of noise reading the newspaper. He kept hitting it in the middle to make it stand straight up in the air, and when it buckled over, he swore and slapped it against the arm of the sofa. I tried to concentrate on my homework at the kitchen table, but made the mistake of saying a vocabulary word aloud, trying to memorize it. I think the word was "infantile." My stepfather sprang out of sofa and charged toward me. He grabbed my arm, pushed me through the kitchen past my mother and through the back door.

About six inches of snow lay on the ground, and I had no shoes or socks on my feet. They were already hurting, beginning to numb in the snow. I looked through the kitchen window at my mother standing inside. She looked back at me through the glass. My stepfather stood next to her and said something in her ear. She put her fists on her hips. He left the room. At first, I was worried that she'd accidentally cut herself with the knife still gripped in one fist. Without realizing it, my own fists rose to my own hips, and we watched each other, mirror images. She laughed then, slowly, as I shivered in the snow. I could no longer feel my feet, what I was standing on. We stood there and stared at each other until I realized that I wasn't standing on anything at all.

Wanda's mother called me at work two months ago. Her voice was loud. I heard the same siren in both of my ears, the one attached to the receiver and the one hanging in the air. "Where are you?" I asked her.

"I'm in the lobby of your office building," she said. "How about lunch?"

"Nancy, its nine-thirty in the morning."

"I'll wait here. They have nice chairs," she said. "When's your lunch hour? I don't want to set you off schedule."

I hurried downstairs to see her. She wore a pink kimono-dress and balanced a wrapped present on her barely exposed knees.

"Happy happy day," she said.

I opened it right there in the lobby, striped paper drifting to the floor. It was a straw hat with purple plastic grapes dangling from one side.

"It's for your head," she said and fell off her heel suddenly. She smiled, drunk.

Down the street, over coffee served in a bowl and beignets, she began to sniffle.

"She won't talk to me, Wanda won't," she said. She pushed at her long hair, distracted. It stayed where she pushed it, as if underlaid with wires.

"What's the matter?" I asked again.

"She doesn't like my house," she muttered. "She doesn't like my boyfriend. She doesn't call him by name; she calls him by number. I think he's Number 35. What could that mean? Oh, I know. She's cruel, she's a Nazi, I brought a cruel Nazi into this world."

"She's not a Nazi, Nancy," I said, nearly mixing the two words up.

"Of course not," she snapped. "She's Jewish."

She was sobering up a bit and settling into her hangover. She wore a real cameo on a chain around her neck.

"These are good," she said, picking up a beignet dusted with powdered sugar.

I bit into one and inhaled sugar, instantly sputtering and coughing. I tried to hold the coughs while I drank coffee, but my diaphragm shuddered against itself, and I blew bubbles into the cup. Wanda's mother walloped me on the back with a well-conditioned palm.

"Snap out of it," she said, and I did, suddenly.

"Sorry," I said.

"Breathe out when you eat," she told me.

"The whole time?"

"Yes."

"But when do you breathe in?"

"When you're not eating," she said.

"Uh-huh."

Suddenly, I looked at her worn face. It was too late for me. And for her.

"You snap out of it, too," I told her, a little too late for context.

She left, as she had the right to do. As soon as she left, there was loss, and there was hunger. I am thirty already, I thought. Thirty. I sat alone at the table for a long time before I finally ate both of our breakfasts, eggs Benedict and trout fried in caper sauce, breathing out the whole time.

But sometimes I think of that last time I saw her, my own mother. Together we visited her mother, Grandma Eloise. My grandmother had experienced a succession of bad men, from her husband who called her "slut" and carried a knife to bed to keep her in line, to her son-in-law who flipped a gun in her face and told her to get out of her own house. Now my grandmother had cataracts and glaucoma. She usually just sat all day in a chair faced away from both the window and the television set. She also had Alzheimer's but recognized some voices, not mine. My mother's voice sliced through the stale afternoon. It glanced off the rusted legs of furniture and the ceramic angels rimmed with dust.

"Guess who can't even wash her own dishes?" my mother said. "Guess who can't manage to keep her drawers clean?"

"Me, me," said my grandmother.

My mother's mouth formed a tightly pressed smile as she slapped the frozen lasagna onto a cutting board. My grandmother flinched at the noise.

I put my hand on my grandmother's shoulder, but it gave at the pressure like bread dough.

On the way home, my mother clasped her gloved hands above the steering wheel.

"I can't believe you did all that," I said.

"All what?"

"What if I do that to you when you're old?" I asked her. "How would you feel?"

She shrugged.

"What happened to you?" I asked.

"What do you mean?" She looked down at her thin coat, her lap.

"How did you get so bitter?"

Her face pursed up. "Listen to you, the big pop psychologist." Her voice caught a little.

Thinking she was hurt, I lowered my voice. "Is it because of your marriage?"

"You're unfit to talk about my marriage. You're the reason I'm alone today."

Staring at the mile markers and the dead scenery, I heard myself say, "You're no kind of mother. You're not my mother."

I turned my head to look at her. Tears poked out of the corners of her eyes, catching in the wrinkles. I was so sorry. And I wasn't sorry at all. Past her head, the world shot past too quickly for me to register it. Then it stopped as she pulled over and parked on the side of the road. She left the car running as she took off her gloves.

She grabbed my left hand and aligned it with hers, palms facing us. They were perfectly identical—like twin maps. Lifeline, love line, the same creases in the thumbs. The crooked forefinger. All the same lines and cracks waiting to happen.

"Ha," she said. I shook my head and tried to pull my hand away. She just gripped it tighter and turned toward me quickly. Her warm breath pushed against my face until I thought I would faint.

"If I'm not your mother," she asked, "then who the hell are you?"

Overture

for Gabriella

There had been a cricket in the basement
when I dreamt you were an unopened envelope on my chest.
I heard on the radio how silverware suddenly tarnishes in a drawer
before disaster, tornadoes, sudden changes in weather.
The voice on the radio, on the lookout, she said, "It's beautiful...
it's not dark... it's good." Meaning the silverware.

For weeks we watched your heart
your breath, dip and peak and wander along the screen.
The week we brought you home, they found the long-gone
missing woman's body while deer hunting in one of the western
counties under the year's first snow
　　　—every valley shall be exalted.

The television vet spoke of the jealous dog
swallowing all of its owner's jewelry whenever she left,
even the dreamed-after diamond tennis bracelet.
I saw a bee-bearded man, listened to Tchaikovsky's span of months
and to a piece of music called the "Silken Ladder Overture,"

and just as finely were we ascending to some place past
the blurred coming-home-from-the-hospital photograph, beyond
even sight of our selves. I dreamt someone asked
for a lock of *my* hair in a world of perfectly
cloned sheep, of "silver needles" tea beneath

the all-throated prize finches. A blood and primrose world—
my darling—a white-tea-of-leaf-buds world, mild as your first tears.
When you sleep beside me, my arm locks across you.
Oh, how we'll whirl and circle, be whirled and fear-throated
a breathless carnivalesque, a ride of spinning cups.

Peking Robins

At night you wake, not to seek me
but to come to your self, a small song—
here is your hand on the wall
in the squares the porchlight makes.
You are the day's hard rain. It becomes you
(and all the clouds in the pond).
Tonight the fox is struck, the steeple
reaches up but does not shine.
The town clock continues as your familiar.
Midnight and you wake, become the Peking Robins
restless from perch to perch at the bird shop.
You in tissue stained glass hanging darkly
centered in the window. You are that decoration:
the paper plate, its glittered rim, its glittering rim.

You Open Your Hands

You learned the intimate—
to recognize faces,
latch on to the breast,
cry out your pain,
smile into a smile

—and you held that knowledge close
in your strong reflexive grasp,
as if under your fingers,
those tender miniatures,
a secret lay at the center of your palm.

Now you unfist your hands
and reach into vast air,
pat flowers on the pillowcase,
fan your fingers across my breast,
find you can touch as well as be touched.

As when we were one,
your body still nestles in mine—
(belly skin meets belly skin, eye meets eye).
Soon your fingers will pull the world
in close to taste, to see

—for you demand I turn you outward
to encounter constellations of faces,
bright slabs of window light.
Oh, small child,
all that patterns and shines mesmerizes you,

and you open your hands!
I see how beautifully,
with shudders of excitement,
you enter the open cosmos—
and, in nearly invisible increments,

part from our close circle—

What to Tip the Boatman?

Delicate—the way at three she touched
her hands tip to tip, each finger a rib
framing the teepee of her hands.
So tentative that joining, taking
tender hold of her body, as if the ballast
of her selfhood rested there. Already
she could thread tiny beads through the eye
and onto string, correctly placing
each letter of her name, sorting
thin black lines to make an alphabet,
the needle just so in her little hand.
She loved that necklace less
than cat's cradle, a game to weave
the strand through forefinger, ring finger, pinkie.
She could lace a basket, a boat
that could even carry water. What to tip
the boatman? I asked, trying to amuse her
with church and steeple turned to my empty palm.
Naptime, she'd lie there making shapes
above her, signing the air.

Later I saw the light touch in those twinned
fingertips had become her way
of holding still, keeping balance.
She had reached home before I did, finding
no mother at the bus stop, and entered
the silenced house for the first time alone.
Ancient, venerable, the whole place
waited, a relative with smells and creaks
she hesitated to greet. When I found her
she had made her way to the formal great room,

polite center of the hectic house where even
the clock's old thud gave back the heart
of simple waiting. Good guest, a shadow
on the rose Victorian settee, she sat,
her hands precise before her, an offering.

Those Alternate Sundays

for Kiernan

when my daughter's tugged
    home—diminishing yellow skull
        a balloon blown beyond the western

pond—the raspberry tang of shampoo
    seeps into pillows and futon;
        her tuneless whistle needles the hall;

the torn, lacy hem of her soul
    nestles among Victorian dolls
        strung in hammocks along one wall.

Porcelain faces press bright webbing.
    Come here, I beckon the leaf-wisp...
        Come down, I urge, as if tempting

a hummingbird with a fingertip's
    blister of nectar...and when
        I exhaust myself and sleep,

the summoned transparency
    burgeons, puffing the rumpled
        bed's canopy, then softening

the wintry pane with our common
    breath, willing my daughter to return
        to murmur her secret name.

Fragments

When I smashed the plastic Barney plate
to smithereens, bashing it over and over
against the slate rim of the sink as yellow shards
flew all over the kitchen floor, the children
were upstairs, and I was thankful
they hadn't seen me like that, or been scared.
I could sweep up everything, through a smear
of tears, and forget anything had happened.

But that isn't what has happened.
Not long after that, we moved away
from the old clapboard Colonial we owned
in a hamlet among hayfields and cow pastures,
and though I already look back on our time there
with a nostalgia like green fields in spring,
something inside me as jagged as those fragments
won't let me forget I was happy

and unhappy at the same time, that the blessings
of the domestic can founder in a loneliness
as deep as the snows of our first winter,
which mired the house. The moments
of joy have been faithfully recorded
in acid-free albums and the pages
of two baby books, but what about
the stretches of despair, the sudden rages?

They're lodged like shrapnel that cuts from inside
when my mind suddenly moves the wrong way,
late at night, for instance, when I can't sleep:

a memory of our son and daughter laughing
and jumping from square to square on the kitchen floor
we painted ourselves in a check pattern
abruptly interrupted by that plate
shattering against the unforgiving slate.

Gray Girl

The year my father's molar disintegrated was also the year my half brother died. The two were related. "Willpower!" my father said. "I *will* keep my tooth from decaying." But decay it did. Every day he'd show us his molar as proof of the immense powers of his will. We saw the hole grow bigger, work its way down the side of the tooth, eat into my father's gums.

"Why is the word 'gums' plural?" said my youngest sister. She was very literal that way.

My father was not my mother's husband. Her husband was gone, somewhere. I had called her husband "Dad," and now I called my father "Dad." I had called other men "Dad." I had fathers coming out of my ears.

My mother used to evaluate men with a number: "sixty" (said disparagingly); "forty" (said with disgust); "seventy-five" (said with some interest); and, rarely, "more than a hundred." She was talking about how much money she thought they made, in thousands. She used to collect money memorabilia, things like a paperweight with a dollar bill preserved in glass, and a pillow with "Love is nice but get the ice" embroidered in red thread. On the living room wall hung a picture of Ginger Rogers looking like a goddess and wearing faux coins over her breasts and groin.

My mother looked younger than her age—"That's the single biggest advantage of being Japanese. Are you memorizing this?"— and her skin was gold and flawless and radiated with what I can only call invitation. In fact, my three half sisters and I were memorizing her every word. My half brother, Raymond, didn't have to memorize anything, since he would grow up to be the hunted, not the hunter. As such, he was both more special and less interesting than us girls.

My mother kept her jewelry collection in a safe deposit box. When I was thirteen, she took me and my older sister Marilyn to the box to look at its contents. Perhaps I remember it as more grand than it was. But to me it was splendid, and it was all appraised, the occasional phony parceled out to Goodwill or the Salvation Army. "Even poor women like to look nice," said my mother. "A man who gives a woman a fake diamond is not a man at all," she said. "It'll all be yours when I die, girls." She said this last in a cooing voice. At the bank I picked up the heavy gems and weighed them in my hand. It was as if I were weighing my future. She said her collection was worth "a hundred." She took a bracelet from my hands and turned it in the light. She gazed at Marilyn and me proudly as we leaned against each other, gaping. "You understand," she said softly. "I can tell you do." She clasped a strand of pearls around Marilyn's neck. She and Marilyn admired the pearls, which looked strangely like a shiny noose around my sister's throat. My mother suggested we each take one item home, to spend the night with.

At home later, I sat in the bathtub for an hour wearing only a diamond bracelet while my sisters pounded on the door screaming that they were going to wet their pants. I held up my wrist to the light or laid it on my stomach and watched the diamonds glisten wetly.

I aspired to be my mother, but my mother did not have high hopes for me. Mostly, I was what she called her "little nitwit," because I liked animals, which were "totally useless," and I had only passable manners. She practiced good manners—"A woman without good manners might as well be dead"—but she didn't believe in them. They were just a way of getting another bauble. There were other things a woman might as well be dead without, namely good skin, clear eyes that could lie without blinking, and that certain curve at the waist. She did not believe in exercising because she feared it would destroy that certain curve. Marilyn and I used to spend hours dissecting our mother's every word, and examining ourselves in the mirror, wondering just when we might actually develop the coveted curves. Unlike our mother, we were both skinny girls. Both of our fathers were thin.

My mother was not Raymond's mother. We did not know my half brother well. Over the years, he had stayed the night with us occasionally, when our father and my mother were out on a date. But he had only come to live with us a few months earlier, when Marilyn's dad moved out and my father moved in. We girls secretly used to call Raymond "Mr. Pedestal" because he never had to clean up or learn all the tricks we were learning. All he had to do was watch TV and get straight A's at school. He had first choice every night of which shows he wanted to watch. If we wanted to watch a show, we had to cajole him. The only exception to the first-choice rule was *Hawaii Five-O,* which he always let us watch since he understood the futility of trying to resist the force of four girls screaming at him. He knew girls possessed powers he could not understand. We liked the theme song for *Hawaii Five-O,* and we all planned to live in Hawaii when we grew up. Book 'em, Danno!

My half brother was like a little emperor, soft and rosy-cheeked, smug and imperious, the kind of boy who wouldn't get girls in high school but would marry some pretty little meek thing when he grew up. He watched us while we cooked and told us when to add salt, and how much, and while we scrubbed the kitchen floor he would point out places we'd missed. "*There,* in the corner, a spot!"

While we practiced walking in our room with books on our heads and earrings torturing our lobes, he practiced his French. He was already acquiring my father's stentorian overtones. Every so often, during a gap in the music we listened to, we would hear him demanding, "*Où est la bibliotèque?*" Or, "*Et vous, qui êtes vous?*"

"*Vous, tu, nous,*" we whispered, giggling. Sometimes, to torment him, we'd whisper in his ear, "*Vous êtes le king.*" "*Vous êtes all powerful.*" But he was above that, and ignored us.

My father was one of my mother's few Japanese lovers, and he was taller than her only by virtue of the lifts Marilyn and I discovered in his shoes one day. My father hoped to save my mother from her own depravity, partly with his incipient (and half-hearted) Christianity, but, more importantly, with his understanding of the differences between right and wrong. "Wrong is tricky!" he explained one day over dinner. "Right comes at you straight. But wrong can come from anywhere. From the telephone! From the food in front of you! From delicious food! Sit up straight, Katie." He poked at my shoulder blades, and I sat up. Then he poked at my stomach. "Wrong can come from inside here, and from other places, deep inside you." Evil resided deeply, he said. He nodded knowingly. From the side of my eyes, I could see my sisters looking at me. I knew what they were thinking: "I'm glad he's not my father." But they called him "Dad," too. We all called all our dads "Dad."

I thought I knew what my father meant, but he never asked. I thought he meant that in modern times people are held back by their conventions. They're sneaky bad. They had nice families and stuck their hands down your pants. They had good jobs and made you pay higher rates for their loans. Every so often, my father would ask me or Raymond to explain something he'd lectured on a day or even a week earlier. The trick was, you couldn't just repeat what he'd said. "Explain it with your own twist!" he'd shout. "With your own twist!" So I was ever ready to agitate on the subject of right and wrong, if only he would ask. I was also ready to comment on the Cubs problem, the inferiority of the American League, and the successes and failures of the Chicago school system.

My father was one of those Japanese for whom you could never be American enough. He didn't like us to eat Japanese food. Fish cakes, for instance, were pink, and pink was a come-on, it was a frill, it had no substance. Raw fish was a health hazard. Fermented soybeans! You knew from just looking at fermented soybeans that they were not meant to be eaten.

So instead we ate pancakes, hamburgers, Chef Boyardee pizza, Spaghetti-Os, Campbell's Chicken Noodle Soup—God's food. On special occasions we ate at IHOP. They gave you all the syrup and butter you wanted, and it was real butter, not margarine like we had at home. His only bow to Japaneseness was rice, which he could not live without. In fact, from listening to him talk, you'd think the biggest problem between him and his former wife had been that she fed him potatoes every night.

Meantime, I was screwing my way into hell for sure—with Jimmy Dime, no less. What a name. We screwed in concrete passageways, on the rocks at the beach near the Evanston-Chicago border, and in Susie Fitzgerald's mother's bed. Susie Fitzgerald's mother worked nights, so that was kind of convenient.

My parents did their screwing after they thought we were all asleep, but the extraordinary noises always woke us up. He made love to her with a passion bordering on violence. He was consumed with her. Some nights at dinner, he didn't lecture at all, but merely stared starry-eyed all meal long at my mother.

The first day of summer, my father took us to Grant's Park to see what he called the bums, which is what he called many young people. We had been to Grant's Park many times, but always to see the fountain or the skyline. In fact, we'd been to Grant's Park just that winter, but with another dad. I remembered that we girls wore miniskirts, and bitter cold stung our thighs. Now, in our cutoffs and sandals, we watched the bums. My father was "dressed down" in a stiff golf shirt, golf trousers, and a beret over his crew cut. The bums weren't doing anything, really, but every so often my father would lean in and say to Raymond, "Look at that one." Many of the men admired my mother. Such a beauty crossed almost all lines, Democrat, Republican, bum, executive, man, woman, or what have you.

My father walked with pride as my mother slipped her arm through his. My sisters and I walked behind. Raymond turned around and caught my eyes. He took several Matchbox cars from his pocket. "Here, carry these for me," he said. "They're too heavy."

He handed them to me as my father watched benignly. I knew it would be hard to carry the cars, since my pants were so tight you could not have slipped a playing card into the pockets. I looked to my mother for support. She just smiled sublimely. Did I forget to mention? My father was a rich man. He had his own company, which made shoelaces. Even the shoelaces on the very sneakers I wore to P.E. classes were made by his company, though Marilyn's father had bought the shoes for me at Woolworth's.

My sisters and I walked like princesses following the emperor and his parents. We held our heads high, the way we had learned. Books on our heads. I carried the royal toys.

A strapping young man with hair down to his hips looked at my mother. "Yum!" he said, licking his upper lip. He leaned forward and reached out toward one of her nipples, barely, or maybe not even, touching it. He sat on a bench with several other young men.

My father whipped toward him, startling all of us.

The man's eyes lit up. "Really?" he said with delight. He stood up, ready to fight my skinny little father. But the young man did not understand my father and his inner angers. With the back of his hand, my father slapped him so hard he fell back. Then my father continued to slap him repeatedly. We all watched, stunned, while the man fell to the grass and my father kicked him, over and over, thud, thud, thud.

"Dad!" I screamed when no one else moved. "Dad!" I grabbed at him from behind, pulled at his face. Toy cars flew everywhere. "Dad!"

He came to, straightened out his shirt. The man lay on the ground with his mouth bleeding and a tiny blue convertible next to his ear. His friends leaned over him but looked up at my father. My father turned to my mother. "Are you okay?" he said. *She* was fine. Even the wind had not stirred a hair on her ravishing head.

Later, on the El home, my father said to Raymond, "A man defends his honor." That did not explain the beating. I think my father, insecure about his size and race and even insecure about his insecurity, could not believe this beautiful woman was his, as indeed she was not, nor was she any man's, or, rather, she belonged to all of them who could afford her. One of the loveliest necklaces in her collection was from my father. He walked in her spell, and incidents such as with the young man broke the spell in a way he could not tolerate. There were many things my father could not tolerate.

"Close the door when you enter the bathroom!" my father often shouted. He made us wash our fingernails when we peed. We felt defiled when we pooped. When we pooped, we had to wash especially well. I usually spent the time with the water running while I played with my mother's cosmetics. For my younger sisters, there could be no more toilet humor. This only made such humor all the more precious to them. Whenever I saw them huddled together laughing and whispering insanely, I knew they were making toilet jokes.

And then it happened. First, a car struck Raymond as he walked on the sidewalk. After the accident, I gave him my blood because we shared a rare blood type and because my father did not believe in blood transfusions from strangers. While studying Raymond's blood, the doctors discovered he had leukemia. My father's son, my half brother, the little brat, was sick, and it turned out I possessed the magical marrow. My marrow could save the future emperor, maybe.

"Why me?" I cried to my mother. "He treats me bad!"

"I wouldn't wonder, with such an attitude."

My father shook his head at me. "An attitude like that comes from the darkness deep inside of you."

So I gave my marrow, which I admit was painless; and, later, I gave more blood. My father said Raymond had a rare blood type because *Raymond* was special.

The doctors were shocked at my body's reaction to the marrow transplant and the blood donations. My skin turned pale, then white, then gray. My father wanted to fatten me up, figuring I'd have more marrow that way, in case more was needed. I got chubby, but also grayer. I made my father pay me a dollar a week for standby donation services, and demanded five dollars should another blood or marrow donation be necessary. At first, Raymond's cheeks grew rosy. I admit the color in his bratty cheeks made me feel...something.

At school the other kids called me Gray Girl. I put lipstick on my face, brighter and brighter. I used my mother's amazing makeup palette that could turn her into an angel. I got kicked out of music class for wearing too much makeup. And still Jimmy Dime kept screwing me.

I never ate so much liver. Liverwurst, pâté, liver and onions, chicken liver omelettes, liver and mushrooms, and even, when my father got desperate, raw liver. Chicken liver, turkey liver, calf liver, beef liver, veal liver, and one day goat liver, though where my father got this and what was so special about it I still don't know. My father begged the doctors to take more of my marrow. "It's good marrow," he insisted.

Every morning, I had to get up early to give the room a chance to stop spinning. My fingers and toes got hard and icy, and the skin under my eyes crinkled like an old woman's. My ears rung. The ringing sounded like singing. It sounded like Smokey Robinson. Very pretty. At school I sometimes lost my balance and fell into the lockers while the hallway full of children spun.

My father watched TV with us every night after he got back from the hospital. We watched dramas. Comedies. Good stuff.

But he never noticed. He watched the screen with dead eyes.

Every so often, as much out of curiosity as anything, I accompanied my father to the hospital. One day, we stood in my half brother's room as he slept. I saw something funny in my father's eyes. I'd never seen it before, and couldn't place it. I studied his plain face, trying to understand what exactly I saw. Then I knew: it was love. I stared at my father. He didn't notice me. I'd seen my father's eyes filled with pride, passion, anger, violence, adoration, and worship, but never love. I'd thought his heart incapable.

I'd known for a couple of weeks that I was pregnant, but I hadn't told anyone. I felt fear, dread, and hope. For a moment, seeing my father's love, I thought about telling him of the baby inside me— me, his soon-to-be-fourteen daughter. But I didn't tell him, because I realized the love in his eyes was not meant for me.

My half brother was on a respirator. My father took one of his hands, and motioned me to take the other. My father closed his eyes and began murmuring, "Willpower! You will not die. Willpower! You will not die." I got a weird feeling as I held Raymond's hand, which was even clammier than mine. I felt as if he had also given me blood, as if the same blood coursed through both of us, as if we were Siamese twins. I was him, and he was me. So I think I was the first person in the world to know how lonely he had been in his short life, pointing out spots, reciting his French, friendless except for my father. I was also the first in my family to know he would die very, very soon.

Jimmy Dime got a car that winter. It didn't run, but it was good for screwing, if we kept our parkas on. There was a long seat in back, and I could stretch myself out fully, or fold my flexible legs up over my head as Jimmy pounded. After the first time in the car, we lay contentedly afterwards. "I'm getting fat," I said.

"There's just more of you to love," he said. Jimmy Dime loved a good cliché. He kissed my cheek.

It was a cold, cloudy evening. Earlier, walking home from school, I had delighted in the clarity of the blue sky. Now, the clouds hung over the barren trees on Jimmy's street.

"I'm pregnant," I said.

That was what finally made Jimmy Dime want to stop screwing me. Not the avoirdupois, not the gray skin. Those special words,

"I'm pregnant," that have struck fear in the hearts of millions of young men throughout the ages. "It's not mine," he said, and that was the last time I saw Jimmy Dime, except spinning through the hallways with the other kids.

I lay on the car seat and let the cool air caress my knees. In truth, silly me, I felt I was ready to be a mother.

Jimmy Dime shouldn't have worried. A couple of weeks later, I lost my baby at Susie Fitzgerald's apartment. I was walking home one evening from the Reach Out Center, where kids went "to keep off the street," when a pain in my stomach staggered me. I struggled to Susie's, pounding on the door. She let me in, though she had been screwing Frank Delamo—who was a minor celebrity because his father's second cousin played in Johnny Carson's band—on the living room couch. Frank gazed at me dazedly from among the leopard-skin cushions. I stumbled into Susie's mother's familiar room, and collapsed onto the bed. Susie followed me in, worried. "Are you drunk?" she asked.

"Yes, drunk," I said.

Then she seemed annoyed. "That bedspread cost fifty dollars," she said. "If you're going to throw up, please please go into the bathroom." So I got up and had my miscarriage instead on Susie Fitzgerald's mother's bathroom floor. I took off my skirt and panties and felt the sticky blood spread down my thighs. I cried. I prayed. I wanted God, but would have accepted the Devil. But nobody came to me. My blood trickled down my legs and onto the tile. I thought I could hear my mother saying, "When you dine out, protect your clothes from stains." I carefully moved my skirt away from the blood. The tile was cold on my cheek. A funny feeling came over me, unlike any feeling I'd ever had before. I concentrated, trying to place the feeling. Disconnected words entered my mind: God...blood...pâté. And then I thought, Why me? Not, why could only I save my brother? Rather, why could I not save him?

Why?

The day he died what was left of my father's tooth fell out. He didn't even notice. Would a dead man notice if a tooth fell out?

Later that night an eerie silence fell over the city as the first blizzard of the season hit. It seemed like the quietest blizzard I'd ever been in. Years later, I lived in Los Angeles. After the riots of 1992, and the earthquake of 1994, I knew similar eerie silences. These silences reminded me of that night my brother died, of the sound of my father sobbing all night in the bedroom. I have never heard such sobs, animal-like groans that came from somewhere deep inside of him where I thought only wrongdoing resided.

The clock glowed orange.

At three in the morning, I heard my mother in the kitchen, and I got out of bed and went to her. My father still sobbed in the background. I don't know what I wanted to say. My mother, still dressed, was heating milk. Finally, I said, "Mom, have you ever been happy?"

She stroked my face and spoke gently. "I have bigger fish to fry," she said.

I went back to bed, lying in the quiet that was broken only by my father's sobs, and thought about the men who had loved my mother, how for years they came and came, like locusts. How eager they were to have their hearts broken, their egos crushed. Some of them were really nice. I mean, really and genuinely. Others stuck their hands down our pants. I thought about my brother, his straight A's and his Matchbox cars that he played with alone for hours. It was getting light out. Still my father sobbed. What were these fish my mother had to fry?

Gray skin, bums, locusts, diamonds. Wrong, right. I was half-asleep. At some point, my father stopped sobbing. Spaghetti-Os. The silence was finally complete. Finally, silence.

Sickle

Sharper than the scythe, which, like the ladder
and the boards I couldn't lift, was long.
And quicker, since it was smaller,
and, swung in an arc, would sing.
I was the age of Latin in school, *mollis*
for mullein, the flannel of whose leaf
girls would rouge their Quaker cheeks with,
for whom vanity, even beauty, was a wildflower.
Weeds are waste, like the milkweed's semen milk,
and this was work that I could do, through
afternoons the sun would drive
your bare head into your shoulders.
Then a need for salt and the spilling
of some blood, blisters and exhaustion,
lacerate missed chances, biblical water poured—
carrot lace and goldenrod swept
to the ground like harvest, star-thorn
Canada thistle cut to the rose at the root.
I used the sickle because the scythe
was too much weight, and because death's
instrument, on the shoulder of the monk's head's
hood-and-mantle, looked too much like it.
You wanted, when you were finished, a field.

The Spell

Everything rots but flowers leave memories.
I was the boy who loved flowers, dried, fresh,
not just their fragrance but their bee-stung
bodies prayerfully folded into dusty skin.
I was the boy who walked limp-limbed, scent-drunk,
with the smell of spit on my hands, swearing:
Relinquish me of my desire
to be sunlit, beautiful.

They sat in vinegar water, blooming
past their time, their mouths open, white roaring
tigers perched high on the mantle top
in the robe room, down in the church cellar—
I moved swiftly on my tiptoes, stealing
a petal and a stem, wiping dust
from their long, knotty tongues onto my lips.
What was I to do with such big wet lilies?

I was a fire-eater, a witch. I opened
my eyes during the humming benediction
and tipped down to the cellar, stopping time,
dropping the prayer book, its pages fluttering,
and I laid my body in the moist dark
of the robe room, closing the door tight,
eyes not used to the dark, eyes wet, alive
breathing quietly, taking stems in reed-like
halves to wet my lips...

When the deacons found me, their arms reaching,
their faces molded into black masks,
I was honey-eyed, softly burping.
They called out my name in the darkness
of the robe room, and probed my mouth until

the flaking bits and evidence was found
and they whispered in my ear:
Girls have names like flowers...

Boys have names you can yell...
What is your name? Do you know your name?
But all my secrets were silent and heat
flowed through me like fire in glass.

Sunspot

I think I will become a selfish man.
That's what it will take to purge myself
of my sick need to give. Strong is stubborn,
many-limbed, but single-minded. Alone.
I think I will be just like Eric was

in boarding school. Early in the morning,
when insomniacs sit awake, I
would watch him running hard around the track,
my face and hands pressed to the window.
Four years after I was raped and I still

could not sleep. I saw, with the rising sun
easing up to join Eric's incessant
circumambulation, a high school track
star, brown and beautiful on his early watch.
And I knew, morning after morning at

the window, that I could love him, be more
than running could to him, could give myself
completely only four years after I
was raped. And when I came to know Eric,
write his student government president

speech (he won), blow him, wash his clothes every
Sunday, I learned how strong the beautiful
are, how selfish. How alone. How hard they
run, sunstruck down the stretch. I will be Eric.
I will take what is given and be gone.

Trees

One summer he planted a tree
it was young, just a few branches
no bigger than a rosebush.
We were intent on watching it
we were young
we wanted the fruit to come.

Father brought the coffee can outside
paced between the tree and the backyard spigot.
We liked to watch him fill the can
feed water to the little tree.
We liked to see the brown soil
blacken beneath his fingers.

Young trees keep their fruit inside
for so long.
You have to stay with them
for years before
they'll bear it.

When the first pear came
we forgot about the water
and the soil and the man
with the coffee can.
We could already taste
its sweetness through the hard, green skin.
It hung there new,
like so many curves we recognized.
Don't touch
he said
don't touch.
We listened at first, we obeyed
because it was small then

easier to resist
but later we could see
its size would fill up our hands
and at night when he went away
we held it.

Finally, the yellow ink took over
the flesh was soft
we became gentle.
Father decided it was time
to pluck it
he decided it was
time to eat.

Mother brought out the special plate
the red one mottled with Chinese birds.
He placed the yellow pear on the red plate
divided the fruit with a knife.
It lay there open like a flower
a pale tropical thing with four
petals, keen with the smell of sugar
each one dripping juice, almost tears
each one, riven from the others,
so yellow against the red birds.

Choose one
he said
and we knew he would watch
to see which one we chose.
The old story was thickly printed in the air
he did not have to speak
to tell it
the story of the child with the most honor
the one who saves the best
for her mother.
All of us fight
for the smallest piece.

Soon the fruit is gone
eaten under his watchful eye.
Time to wait for the next one.
Mother rinses the plate
shines the birds with her swift cloth.

Now he has cut the tree down.
He says it interferes with the plumbing
too many roots.
Mother is a bird flying.
Sister sends me fruit in the mail:
dried apricots, cranberries, apples, plums.
We are young, small
hungry as squirrels,
hiding our fruit in the cupboards.

D. NURKSE

The Play Hour

1. The Sandbox

We celebrated a funeral
for a dead ladybug
and smoothed the surface
with the belly of a spoon.

Who would count the tiny dots
now, or study the long crawl
and sudden flight?

We dug a pit
for a hemlock leaf
curled into itself.

We said last rites
for a fleck of mica—
who'd watch it flash
at evening as if to hint
at a powerful secret?

We buried our hands
up to the wrist.
The dark no one sees
bit under our nails.

But we wouldn't wait long:

The sparrow arrived
just out of reach
to hold us safe
in a bright indifferent eye.

2. *The Swing*

Happiness made us sad.
Sadness was ecstatic.
When we soared
we longed to plummet.
We rose to sunset
side by side, Converse Hi-tops
aimed at faint Venus.

Dad pushed
and puffed on his pipe,
nearer, more remote,
as the yard assembled itself
delicate with distance:

dusky dog, twilight cat,
dazzling kitchen window
where Mom peeled a carrot
and stared at shadows.

Why were we so lonely?
At last we felt no one
behind us and slowly
returned amazed to earth.

3. *The Seesaw*

Perfectly equal
we wait for wild laughter
to lift one and let the other
run sobbing from the game.

Cicada

For a week it's been spinning
the tale of a thing
about to believe
its new body.
Today the eyes are gone,
the center split
where form sidestepped
its own riven length.

That's just likeness
hinged to the tree.
A souvenir.
A transparency.

To find it now
make a space in the ear
in the shape of what it's become:

A thirst.
A flood.

Listen. Already
the ear
is the lip
of a generous cup.

An Arithmetic

Because the world insists on still giving and giving at six,
mastering addition seemed its natural complement,
a kind of cataloguing the earth's surplus.
I loved the fat green pencil
shedding graphite as I pressed rounded
threes, looping eights into the speckled
yellow newsprint. Loved, too, the sturdy,
crossed bars of the plus sign, *carrying over*
in stacked columns of double,
triple digits: the plump sums I'd *arrive* at.

Subtraction proved another sort
of reckoning. First I had to learn
to *take away* (apples or pennies pictured
in the workbook), then settle
for the solace of a *remainder.*
I've never wanted less of anything—money, food
or love—but over time,
have come to understand the process:
like any human calculation,
the *difference* being
between what I have wanted
and what I got.

The World I Painted Twenty Years Ago

The angle of the postman's cap
looked like he'd dressed himself in dark,
the darkness, say, that's lurching from
his mouth, where teeth should be, a smile
like charcoal, awkward on this full-
grown man, but safer for his world
where fuchsia picket fences float
above a lumpy car that trails
a cautious, chastened string of smoke
in pencil lines behind it, up
the two dimensions of a hill
toward a listing cabin with
a crescent smirk and eye-dots in
the window, magnified in each
small feature, shown the way those eyes
would see: noticed, loved, critiqued,
then naturally forgiven, since
the failing is a piece of the
extenuating circumstance,
this sharing of the blunt
but friendly, scored, veined,
imperfect anvil of the earth.

Centipedes on Skates

L ast week we had a riot. Pomo, my boyfriend, tried to kill him-
self with a pencil. Everybody freaked. Then eight pigs rushed
in and beat the crap out of us. I got put into The Coat. I hate
being put into that thing. You can't breathe. It smells like piss and
shit. Though I couldn't move a muscle, I kept on screaming until
they stuck a needle into my neck. Then I blacked out.

For the next few days I said nothing to nobody. Just sat in my
cell and stared at the wall in front of me. Vomit-green. I was told
my mom came to visit while I was in that state, but I don't
remember. They told me I talked gibberish while she was here.
Maybe. But I don't trust anything they say. Not after what I've
seen them do to Pomo, and the others.

I've got to get out of here.

I got sent here by my mother and my shrink. I was mutilating
myself, and had suicidal thoughts, they said. I had no choice. I'm
seventeen, a minor girl.

We go to daily group therapy sessions in the Bubble Room to
work on our "issues." Sometimes we just talk. Sometimes we just
jerk off. And sometimes they give us number two pencils to fill in
bubbles. The bubbles are possible answers to questions we've
been given. Questions like, "If you were an animal, which of the
following would you be?" or "In a garden, do you see yourself as a
flower or a bee?" Asshole questions like that. But after Pomo's act,
they don't give us questions that require pencils anymore.

Therapy sessions are bullshit. They just want to control you.
That's what this place is all about. The only time the sessions
are any good is when others say what they want, or just let you
zone. But every time things start getting good, they send for the
pigs.

They don't like Pomo. They don't like him because he speaks
his mind and doesn't take their crap. And when they try and shut
him up, he fights back. Once they told him to shut up, and he got
up quietly, walked over to the wall, and peed. They don't like

Pomo. They don't like you having boyfriends in here. But they'll never separate us.

Thursday's session was different. It was about triggers. The head shrink, Dr. Norads (Dr. Gonads to us), explained that triggers are things that happen just before you start using. It can be anything. Smell, an overheard conversation, a face, an old movie.

We were in a circle. The guy sitting next to me, an older guy named Fast, told how he got on speed. Pomo laughed. He said, "That's a great title. How Fast got up to Speed."

Fast was a Vietnam vet and during the war worked as a "tunnel rat." He and some other rats, high on skag, found a tunnel used as both a hospital and ammo dump. It smelled to him of chlorine "like there was a hot tub nearby." Below they found three "VC nurses" and raped them. When they were done, they jammed hand flares up them, watched their eyes bleed and bellies bloat to incredible size, then explode. After, they set fuses and blew up the tunnel. He'd never used speed before that day, and got hooked on it because he was afraid to dream at night after the incident. Now every time he smells chlorine or sees pictures of tunnels he wants to use. Today, he told us, he can't go underground or in a subway, or go through a long tunnel on the highway. One time, in a taxi, he got caught in a traffic jam in the Callahan Tunnel in Boston and freaked. He started screaming, then foaming at the mouth. They had to bring an ambulance to get him out of there. He almost died.

Fast broke down and cried at times during his story. The guy sitting next to him, Bobby Wayne (I asked him his last name during orientation and he said, "Something or Other"), kept saying "Christ Christ Christ Christ Christ Christ Christ" the whole time he spoke.

We all had to give our triggers that day. By the end of the session, we were jumping out of our skins.

Last night Bobby Wayne Something or Other got matches from somewhere and torched his Bible. The Bible caught his bed on fire. Smoke alarms woke us. We were led into corridors and down exits smelling of burnt linoleum. Fire trucks came moaning into the street where we stood. Everyone stared at smoke pouring out of a third-story window. A patient standing next to me, named Church Ortiz, said, "Last night I turned into a very large black woman."

Bobby Wayne was strapped onto a stretcher and placed in the back of an ambulance with three men dressed in whites. He was saying, "Lamb of the Lord, forgive them for they know not what they do."

The next day I got transferred to the adolescent psych ward. Everyone there was my age or younger. Unlike my old ward, there were no great stories by Vietnam vets. We sat in circles as before, but no one spoke. Unlike the other place, they were shy here. After a time, I liked the silence. I never spoke in the Bubble Room. Now they leave me alone. Pomo wasn't moved with me, although he's around my age. I miss him every day.

I miss a lot of people. My friends mostly. I'm not allowed any visitors but my mom, and I don't want to see her. She's the reason I'm here.

Since I moved here I've had this regular dream. I'm in a car with friends from my old neighborhood. Though I quit my last year, we're going to our high school reunion. They drop me off at a theater in Boston to get seats. As we pull under the marquee, there's an explosion at the end of the street, at the top of a building. We look. There is one of those enclosed walkways connecting buildings. There is fire and smoke. Large glass windows explode and shatter into pieces and fall into the street. Bodies tumble out, their fall broken by a mass of crossed electrical wires that are somehow strung across the street at each story. Three of the bodies, young males, land on their feet like cats and stumble toward our car. They are badly burned. One of them says, "I didn't want to hurt this way." They approach us, then collapse in the street. Their lifeless bodies sprawl around the car. Just then, out of nowhere, cops arrive and begin dragging the bodies away. As he drags a charred, smoking victim onto the sidewalk, a cop turns to me and says with a faint smile, "This is a liar, young lady."

I've been locked up in this ward for one month and three days. And five weeks in the other ward.

I've got to get out of here.

On Monday they took us outside. Since I've been no trouble they promoted me to Level III, and you get to go on outings.

They took us to Harvard Square in a hospital van, fed us at Au Bon Pain, and shepherded us around the Square with no clear direction. People stared at us like we were retards from a group home. We walked past the T-stop, and I looked down into the Pit to see if any of my old buddies were there smoking a butt, but it was still morning, too early for any of them to show.

Later, however, as we rounded Nini's Corner, I felt a tap on my shoulder and turned. It was one of my Pit buddies, Tania.

"Where the fuck you been?" she said.

Tania had a nose ring, an eye ring, and a navel ring. When I last saw her, she was going to get a ring on her tongue. She helped me put in my nose ring, and another into my navel. I was into body piercings. I cut an anarchy symbol into my arm. I wrote a paper on it at school. I cut some more. I watched myself bleed. That's when they hauled me away.

"Been locked up," I said. I pointed at the group. "With them."

"What the hell for?"

"For being bad," I said. I thought my face formed a smile, but was unsure.

"Being bad at what?"

"At life."

"Wanna go over to Hector's?"

I looked around me and saw that our group leader, Serge, and others were absorbed in the magazines at the newsstand. No one was watching me.

"Yeah," I said. "Let's go."

We left unnoticed.

We went over to Hector's, but nobody was home. I bought us snow cones with some of the pocket money given me by the hospital. We walked to the Charles River and sat on the cement railing of the bridge. We watched crew teams glide across the water. They moved so gracefully. That was the way I wanted to pass through life. Gliding along, nothing touching me.

"They look like insects," Tania said, tossing her paper cone into the water below. "Centipedes on skates."

It was dark when we got to Hector's. Hector Perez lived with Ruben Lopez and Dan Villanueva. They were all home. I didn't know Hector well, only met him a couple of times. He'd been one of my suppliers. I didn't know his roommates and had never been to his apartment. He lived on the third floor of this building just off Mass. Ave.

Just as we arrived, Dan and Ruben were going out to buy some Rastafarian pot. I gave them all I had on me, three dollars and some change, to put into the pool. Tania had said they had Toad Slime, but all they really had were ludes and some peyote. I took some ludes, washing them down with Southern Comfort. Later, when they returned with the pot, I smoked a few joints. Hector put on 2 Live Crew, and we all tried to dance rap. Everyone bounced as if shook by invisible hands. I didn't know if I was moving right; I just raised my knees as high as I could, and brought them down. I felt like I was marching in place.

After a while, I saw Tania go into the bedroom with Hector and Dan. I went into the kitchen. I leaned over the sink and hurled my guts out. Ruben stood beside me the whole time. With one hand he rubbed my back in a circular motion; he kept saying, "There there there there there there." When I was done, he took a large serving spoon and pushed the vomit around the sink. It was solid and held together. He said, "Whaddya say I cook this, and we freebase the fumes?"

When we got back in the living room, Ruben changed CDs and put on Seal.

"For mood," he said. "We can scat."

I sat in a sofa chair clutching my stomach. I could hear moaning coming from the bedroom. "I gotta go," I said.

But Ruben grabbed my arms and pulled me out of the chair. "Dance w'me, dance w'me," he said.

He pressed hard against me, and cupping his hands around my ass, lifted me off the floor, carrying me backward. It seemed I was airborne a long time. When I came down, he had backed me against the air conditioner. It was like déjà vu. I was in the past, a time traveler.

"You give head?" he said.

"I gotta go," I said again, trying to think of where that was. His breath and body smothered me. I couldn't move or breathe. I was sick.

With one hand on my chest, he pinned me while he fumbled

with his fly. He got his cock out and held it in his hand. It was small and limp. He shook it, and the more he shook it, the angrier he got. He said, "C'mon c'mon c'mon c'mon." It looked like a fat dead worm.

Finally, he let go of it and shouted, "Eat my balls, you little fucking cunt."

He raised the hand that had held the worm and made a fist.

I felt myself falling sideways before I felt the hurt on my jaw. The word "dive-bomber" came into my head.

"You must have blacked out," Tania said.

When she found me the next morning, I was lying on the floor, my head resting against the doorjamb to the kitchen. My neck hurt from lying that way all night. My head throbbed. There was blood.

"You've been bleeding," Tania said. "Your lip's cut. Your shirt has blood from it. What happened to you?"

"I fell," I said, getting up. I went into the bathroom and wiped my lip with a washcloth. There was nothing I could do about the shirt. I found some Darvon in the cabinet and swallowed a couple with water.

Tania followed me into the bathroom. "Did that pig hit you?"

"We had a fight," I said. "He said he was sorry, though." Lying came naturally to me. I did it without thinking whether I'd be believed or not.

"Don't take their shit, Leila," she said. "You don't have to."

"Where is everybody?"

"Gone," Tania said. "I just got up. Nobody's here. We've got the place to ourselves."

"I want to go." Right then, I really missed Pomo.

"Do you want to go to Cafe What?" she said. "We can stop at my place and get you another shirt."

I shrugged. "Okay."

Somehow, along the way, we never stopped at Tania's to get a shirt. We got on the subway and rode to Boston, getting off near Newbury Street. Tania had money for tokens. It turned out Tania had lots of money. If she didn't have money, she'd always get it. She either stole or fucked for it. Most times she had more money than anyone I knew.

The sky was low with clouds the color of bruises. We hung out for a while in Copley Square and bought reefers from some wiggers, before going down to Condom World. Tania was always buying condoms. Blue and red and green and transparent ones. I never knew if she got anyone she slept with to use one. I think she just liked having them.

When we came out of Condom World we ran into Mike Streeter. He looked almost the same. Still had the goatee beard and ponytail, but something was different. I didn't notice it at first, until Tania whispered to me as we started up the street with him, that the top of his right ear was missing. He still wore his ring there, though I thought this would only call attention to it.

"We're going to Cafe What?," Tania said. "You want to come?"

"Yeah," he said. "Yeah, I could use a drink. What do they have on draft there?"

"They don't sell liquor," Tania told him. "It's just a coffeehouse."

"Hah!" he said. "Like hell they don't."

"They really don't," I said. "We couldn't get served, anyway. We're minors."

"Don't fool yourself," he said, and gave a knowing laugh and wink. "Bread gets buttered. It's business."

Cafe What? was crowded. Tania and I ordered first. I got lemon water and pita bread, and she got an espresso. We told Mike we'd save him a place at our table. We got one nearby the counter. Close enough to watch him order. "This I gotta hear," Tania said.

"What do you have on draft?" he asked.

"I'm sorry, but we don't serve beer, sir," the woman behind the counter said.

"C'mon," he said. "Don't give me that."

"I'm serious," she said. "We don't serve beer. This is a coffeehouse."

"I'm supposed to believe everyone in here's drinking coffee."

"Or fruit juice."

"Then I'll have a rum and cola."

"We don't serve anything alcoholic," she said. "We don't have a liquor license."

"C'mon," he said, and removed a bill from his pocket. He held it between his fingers and waved it in her face. "Bread gets buttered. It's business," he said, and laughed.

"I'm sorry, sir."

"C'mon," he said. "C'mon, you're not gonna pull that holier-than-thou crap. You're not gonna pull that crap on me now."

"Sir, there are people waiting in line to order."

He hit the counter with his fist.

"Okay, goddamn it," he said. "Give me a goddamn coffee. Black."

"Colombian?"

"Black!"

Mike got his coffee and walked past us. He went into the corner of the room and sat by himself. Tania waved, but he ignored her. He sipped his coffee and stared down at the table.

Tania leaned across our table, her hand cupped to the side of her mouth. She said, "What an asshole, right?"

In the past I came here a lot. I fell in love with a guitar player who played every Tuesday and Thursday. I had it bad for him. I came every day, even on days he didn't play, hoping he might show up anyway. Lemon water and pita bread cost only thirty cents, and you could sit all day. He had a girlfriend, though. She had these nifty tattoos and a nose ring. She played in a band with him, but they, I found out, seldom worked. I got a nose ring and phony paste-on tattoos and sat up front, as close as I could. He always said, "Thank you," and bowed his head when I dropped change into his cup at the end of each performance. Beyond that, we never spoke. After a couple of months, he left and went home to Pittsburgh, a waitress told me. I never saw him again.

"What're you gonna do when you graduate?" Tania said.

"I don't know," I said. The question had no meaning. Though it was just a few months, it seemed ages since I sat in a classroom. I doubted I'd ever go back. I was on the run. But even in school, I never thought about the future. I took each day as it came.

"Dontcha ever think what you might want to do?"

"Yeah," I said. "Sometimes." Once I had thoughts about getting into acupuncture. Holistic medicine. But I had no idea how to go about it. I didn't even know if I'd like it.

"I'd open a store," Tania said. "Selling bonsai trees. With everything going Eastern these days, you could make a killing."

"Totally," someone said at the next table.

"Really," Tania said. "You could do a whole lot worse."

I suddenly felt empty. Hollow. I needed to take something. My head still hurt. I was all red inside. I had the shakes. At any moment I believed something awful was going to happen. I could feel it coming. If I closed my eyes then, I could have seen it. I had to get out of there. But I couldn't move.

"Let's get out of here," I said.

Just then screams erupted. Mike Streeter stood wielding a knife. He had stabbed a woman seated near him, and was lurching forward, stabbing fleeing patrons as he moved. Some men rushed up and tried to take the knife from him, but he slashed them. He then changed to that slashing motion, cutting anyone he could reach. Both arms moved violently. He looked like he was conducting an orchestra. Everyone fell backward, scrambling away from him. A body, a young girl, crashed into our table and toppled it. Tania and I were knocked to the floor. There were more shouts and screams. Mike was suddenly above us. His eyes looked swollen. Tania cursed him. He bent over and slashed her arm, then stabbed my leg. Tania screamed. I stared at my leg and watched a circle of blood form and expand. My mouth opened, but nothing came out. I looked up. I saw him stab another woman, an employee of the café, in the chest, and bolt out the door.

With others, I was taken to the hospital in an ambulance. En route, I passed out several times. I was told that the knife had cut a major artery in my leg. Tania rode with me. She kept saying, "You're gonna make it."

I passed out again as I was wheeled into the hospital, and when I woke up later, I was in a hospital bed, my leg bandaged. I was in a room with four other patients.

Dr. Gonads was there. He wore a smile on his face. It was the same smile he gave when someone in the group started crying. He meant it to show sympathy, but it looked ghoulish.

My mother was there, too. She stood beside my bed, twisting her hands, her face contorted as if fighting back tears. She said, "Why? Why, Leila?"

I stared at a mobile of a moon and stars hanging from the ceiling.

Dr. Gonads spoke to her. He said I was in denial. That I ran away to get revenge and stay in denial.

As he spoke I closed my eyes. I could see myself start to move. Slowly at first. I made a figure eight. Then I glided forward, balancing on one leg, then two. Then many. I accelerated. I felt the wind brush past my body hairs. Things on either side of me blurred as I sped past them.

Respects

Quentin Carter's, little Junie June-Bug's running joke
    was "Where's my quarter,
        you better give me my quarter."

Junie, 12, runt of the 6th grade, School 109, Queen's Village—
    in your face, pest & joker,
        "Where's my quarter,

you better give me my quarter."... This morning,
    police arrested Brian Wright, 16—
        Brian, called a "Herb,"

or dork or nerd, by others in the hood, couldn't stomach being
    picked on & pushed around,

& this time, when Junie jived him, he had a gun,
    pulled it from his jacket:
        "You ready to die?" he asked....

Junie turned, took off too late, Brian fired, missed, fired again,
    caught Junie in the back,

fired again. Junie hit the pavement hard. Brian stood over him,
    shot him again, again,

because, he told the police, the sixth grader hadn't
    shown him "proper respects,"
        had "dissed" him....

Minutes later, from her block of shade trees & swept walks,
    Junie's mother arrived on the scene—

"Oh God, my son," she cried. "Hold on, Junior, don't
    leave me," she cried,
        but the ambulance bore him away,

the paramedics did not power their siren or red light,
    & Wanda Carter knew
        her son was dead....

Today, the spot where Junie died becomes a temporary shrine—
    flowers & votive candles where

his friends stand in that fusion of grief & joy only we
    humans experience when
        violence ruins or ends

somebody else's life. In any case, the Queens DA tells a reporter,
    "It was a mindless, senseless killing.

You've got two kids lost, one dead and one in prison."
    A neighbor says, "Somebody made that gun,

somebody sold it to Brian, our boys are being killed for nothing,
    we've got to get weapons off the street." ...

Where are we? Well, from east of the Apple, now,
    from Long Island's Queen's Village,
        Junie June-Bug sings in our minds,

temporarily—"Where's my quarter, where's my quarter,
    my quarter, you better
        give me my quarter."

At least, according to police, unlike many other young killers,
    Brian does admit
        to feeling some remorse.

Fugue for Kristallnacht

for Angie Suss-Paul

Around the corner where I lived a beautiful synagogue was burning.
Around the corner where I lived. Around the corner.
A beautiful synagogue. Was burning. Where I lived.
Around the corner where I lived a beautiful synagogue was burning.
My father came home in the evening I didn't recognize him.
He didn't want to talk and didn't talk what happened to him.
Was burning. He didn't want to talk and didn't talk.
What happened to him. A beautiful synagogue where I lived.
He didn't want to talk and didn't talk what happened to him.
Will they kill me is not so easy to forget either.
I didn't recognize him. Came home in the evening.
Around the corner where I lived will they kill me. Was burning.
He didn't want to talk. What happened to him.
Will they kill me is not so easy to forget either.
A beautiful synagogue was burning. What happened to him.
We packed the little things what we could carry.
My father said we didn't know where we are going who
will live who will die. He didn't want to talk.
My father came home in the evening I didn't recognize him.
Will they kill me. Around the corner where I lived.
What we would carry. We packed. Who will live who
will die. Around the corner a beautiful synagogue.
I didn't recognize him. My father. What happened to him.
Was burning. Will they kill me is not so easy.
The little things what we could carry. Was burning.
Around the corner where I lived a beautiful synagogue was burning.

If You Wish on Them

Imagine that all you
can do is glitter and you
are only one small star
in an expanse as wide as

infinity is, and surrounded
by a darkness filled up with
other glitterings, fire and
rock making flame into a voice.

And these other small voices
are all you hear in the void,
their cries and shining,
emptiness echoing and emptying

itself in their repetitions
as if, out of loneliness, they
were the only cries for help.
But then you hear other

voices, there beneath you,
fainter, further off, almost
human in their crawlings,
voices out of a sorrow now

earthbound and spinning,
and they say they are wishing
on you, wishing on the flicker
and color of your light,

and, though you have nothing
to offer these creatures, you
want to please them somehow,
so you glitter back prettily.

Stateside

As I walked onto the ward
a soldier's voice rose up tender out of the dusk—
I thought you were my sister.
You have those Irish features.

He was American, a medic during Tet,
whose spirit returned now in spurts
like flames from a clogged gas jet.
Death tanks down the door and your mind

books out of there, comes home shrewd
as an assaulted cat, you'd never guess
the niches it can tuck itself into,
little genius burrows in the merest synapse.

The smell of lemon grass and diesel mingling
in a cloudburst. Quails flushed by
mistake from their ground nest grazing your
cheek. A truck backfiring in your blind spot.

The other guys on the ward
were silent for once.
Irish? he said.
So in my face there it was—

evidence of my secret father
my mother never talked about (as I was
illegitimate).
               After a tropic sunset,

darkness drops *whap* like a
shade snatched down—

but stateside, dusk lingers
as heaven flutters under the earth.

Like a blue pearl, subatomic.
Like a soldier and a nurse, 21 years apiece.
All he wanted was a drink of water
                                        shimmering.

Paraldehyde, She Said

You're a nurse now and this ward ain't the schoolbook,
so you sedate him, paraldehyde, 5 ccs each hip, and don't
expose it to air, it'll turn to vinegar, it'll eat plastic and
it reeks, use a *glass* syringe and DON'T DROP IT. Junkies
howl and sweat and beg but they won't seize and code
like a drunk in DTs. He thinks this is Vietnam. He'll
tear out your throat. Those four-corner restraints keep you
both from getting hurt. Slap him on the hip, he'll jump,
then give your shot, because the slap is anesthetic, so he
won't feel the needle. He struggles, it could break off inside.

Now, you look like you hate to hurt people. But
you're not the first one to stick him, what is he, 23?
Sober him up and he's all yours, 100 percent.
Take him home with you for all I care. But darling—

you better hurt him first.

Happy Birthday

Go ahead. Open it. I think you'll like it.
I made that wrapping paper myself. It's similar to rubber, but not exactly. You kind of have to peel it off. Do you like the avocado color? I bet you've never seen wrapping paper that thick, huh?

Oh, I forgot to tell you—if you touch it in one spot too long it will attach itself to you. Here, let me help you with that—don't panic, now just calm down

Whew. Feisty stuff, huh? You're safe now. As long as no one touches it for the next thirty minutes or so it will die. I know it looks scary writhing about like that, but it can't move around on its own, so as long as we stay out of that corner we're all right.

Pretty neat, huh? I've always wanted to give someone a box inside a box.

Of course not, silly. I've got more taste than that. The box isn't empty.

Look in the corner.

Look closer.

See that strand?

Yeah, the piece of spider web. Pull on it.

I've been collecting webs for the past few months in the woods out back. Then last night I sewed them all into one long strand. Pretty neat, huh?

Keep pulling. It's a long strand.

Keep pulling.

Keep pulling.

You'll see. Your present is at the end of the strand.

Keep pulling.

Keep pulling.

Keep pulling.

Should be sometime soon now. Pretty long strand, huh?

See that door?

Of course it's a door. It's just a very small door. See the door-knob? Go ahead. Open it. Use your thumbnail.

Gee, I'm sorry about that. I guess I should have told you the box behind the door was a big one. Here, let me help you up. Easy there, I've got you. Everything's going to be all right.

See that velvet curtain on the side of the box? Pull it back. There should be an elephant behind it.

Yes, it is a very large red elephant. You don't see many red ones that large. We fed his mother food coloring every day from the time she conceived. Careful, now—don't get too close to his trunk. See that gleam in his eye? We don't call him Mischief for nothing.

Yes, the elephant is on a tightrope. So are we. Don't look down.

It's not much further now, just a hundred feet or so. You can do it, don't quit on me now, breathe (but not too deeply) and don't look down

Good thing you can swim, huh? I never have liked safety nets. I guess I should have told you that the tightrope was that same strand of spider web. We tested it with one person (one *big* person—Horace the Human Landfill), and it held up fine. And of course you and I were doing fine until almost the end—there must have been a weak place in the strand.

Boy, it sure is nice to stretch out on this sandbar, huh? Most people don't know that piranhas sleep for one hour each day. Guess we landed at a good time, huh?

Yes, their eyes were open. They don't have eyelids. I'll have to admit I was a little nervous myself, swimming right by the school like that.

Monkeys. I bet you've never heard anything like *that* before.

So what do you think of the Amazon?

See that little green fern just past your foot? Pull it back.
Can you fit through there? I know it's tight.

Most people don't even know about the root systems of these
trees. There are some pretty good-sized tunnels down here, and
some of them go a long ways. This one comes out in New Mexico.
How 'bout that echo? Pretty neat, huh?

How's that for a view? These mountains are really something.
Smell that fresh air. Wow.

Oh, those are pterodactyls. This is their take-off cliff. Say,
there's our flight now. We'd better hurry or we'll miss him.

Beats the hell out of Delta, huh? I dare say you've never see *this*
sort of excitement before. A blue pterodactyl for two, soaring
through the clouds. Don't be afraid, just hold tight to me. And
don't worry about that screeching—he's just an ornery reptile.

Man, what luck. It just figures that we'd get a shrinking ptero-
dactyl. Oh well, at least we landed in the *South* Pacific, where the
water's warm.

What about this sparkling azure water, huh? Let's take a dive—
there's an old shipwreck over that way just a little bit. Are you
good at holding your breath?

Now look what you've done. I tried to motion for you to leave
the oyster alone, but no, you had to have it your way, you had to
pull the damn thing out of the sand. Congratulations. You've
drained the Pacific Ocean. I certainly hope you're happy.

It seems to me you have yourself a sunbaked ocean bed and lots
of rotting fish. That's what it looks like to me.

I'm going home. I hope you enjoyed your damn birthday. Have
fun with the putrid fish. And don't call me.

White Fang

Hello, readereaper. It's certainly been a while. May I take your coat?

It is four a.m. and my parents and sister are gone to North Carolina for two weeks' vacation, which means I have the house to myself. So:

I come out of the bathroom and the cat is sitting on top of the humidifier (in the hallway, which is carpeted grayly but cleanly). The cat looks at me inquisitively (to be expected from a feline, no?) and says, "Meow?" So naturally I say to my cat, "Meow."

"Mrow," says the cat.

"Mrow," I reply.

"Mraoo." (the cat)

"Mraoo." (me)

"Mrow?" (cat)

"Mrow?" (the me)

"(maoo)." (the feline)

"(maoo)." (yours untruly)

"Mrow?" (the feline again, somewhat more insistently)

"Mrow?" (myself in like manner)

All this time I am petting (the cat). Now she becomes silent. I try a couple more cat words, not knowing what I speak, but Prissy (short for Prissy Grey Bugeater) remains mute. She purrs as I pet her and tell her (now in my own familiar tongue) that I find her somewhat lacking as a conversationalist, but nonetheless refuses further discourse. She is through. So naturally I do the natural thing to do, which is to grab the cat by the midsection and bash her against the wall numerous times until she is quite quite bloody, all the while her making a terrible racket

No, no, not really, silly. I'm just kidding. It was just a joke. I love my cat and would never do anything to hurt her. Really, readerno, I didn't mean it. I'm sorry, okay? Please don't go away.

I teach trombone lessons. That is to say, the children come and sit side by side with me one at a time in a small room (the location of which cannot be revealed for reasons of national security), and we look together at the music stand and I teach. I teach them how to hold the horn and how to blow into it to make it sound good. I teach them how to breathe, how to hold their lips, what to do with their tongue and their right arm, and when they walk into a room to play an audition the first note they play fills the room with a sound the size of God's voice. The walls shake with reboant vibrations and the judges bow down at their feet and beg for their favor and promise that not only they but their children and their grandchildren and their grandchildren's grandchildren will always be first chair junior high Mid-State or first chair All-State (senior high) or whatever the case may be until the end of time, throughout eternity, that on Judgment Day they will be the ones to sound the trumpet calls heralding

Okay, so I exaggerated a little bit. You'll get over it, readerblow. What's that? You want a refund? Too bad so sad. We're here for the duration, whether you like it or not. Hell, we haven't even gotten to the good part yet.

So it's the next afternoon, which for me is morning. At precisely 2:26:34 postmeridian (okay, I know the ":34" part can't be precise, because those things are always changing, and it takes more than one to walk into the kitchen from the hallway), I enter the kitchen from the hallway by foot, at which time I am approached by the aforementioned bug-eating feline.

"Maarraaow," she says.

"Are you hungry, Prissy?" I reply in my standard kitty voice, higher in pitch and somewhat condescending.

"Mraaow!" says the cat. "Maaow? Mraaow?"

"Looks like we're out of kitty food, Prissy. I guess you're out of luck."

"Mraaow?" The cat has a trusting, dependent look on her white-whiskered countenance.

"Maybe if you had made that food last longer, you wouldn't be having this problem now. You should have planned ahead instead of being such a glutton."

"Mraow?"

"That's all there is. There isn't any more. They don't make cat food anymore. They got tired of trying to satisfy rapacious felines such as yourself."

"Mraow?"

"I guess you'll just have to make your own. I hear the Co-op is having a sale on bone meal this week. If you leave now you can probably make it there before they close."

So then of course I fed the cat, after which I fed myself, after which I went into the living room and lay on my back on the purply carpeted floor and masturbated, after which I called my senator and demanded that the American public be protected from stories such as this, most especially my mother and father and the forty-two children I will someday have with my beautiful intelligent loyal caring wife if I can ever find her in time before it's too late

Sometimes when a young student is neglecting his practice I will tell him that if he continues to do so there will come a day when I step over to the wall and push my secret button (hidden cleverly in the baseboard), at which point in time a trapdoor will open beneath the student and he will fall down into the alligator pit below with all my other students who failed to practice, never to be heard from again. At this point the sixth-grader's eyes usually get a little bigger, although he is of course old enough to know I am only kidding.

I call our dog White Fang now. Her real name is Loretta Lee (my mother's doing, certainly not mine), but a few nights ago (actually many nights, several months, maybe a year or more, who knows, time passes slowly when one has a college degree and is almost thirty and resides with one's parents), she began to howl. It was tentative howling, testing the waters if you will, and short-lived seeing as how I stepped from my room and told her to cut it out, but all the same I found it amusing and so now I call her White Fang.

So the local community band played a concert recently about thirty miles away, a Christmas concert. Some of the younger members rode with some of the older members, including an eighth-grade student of mine that rode with me. On the way to the concert we listened to Mahler's Fifth, played by the Chicago Symphony, and when the tape got to the first heavy-duty trombone passage, one of those apocalyptic kind of things so common with Mahler and the trombone, one of those licks that choke me up half the time because I want to play like that so badly, I looked over at him through the winter night darkness inside the truck, and I could see that he was hit. I could see in his bespectacled face that the sound had moved him, grabbed him deep inside and changed him. Like I knew at that moment that someday he would take Friedman's place as principal trombone of the Chicago Symphony. But then we played the concert and he plowed through key changes like a bull in a china shop. Which still doesn't mean anything, really, I mean he's only in the eighth grade and he can already play a three octave E-flat scale, far up into the land of treble clef, and sometimes he gets a *really* big sound

Sorry, readergo. I almost let that one get away from me. I'll try not to let it happen again. I promise. You have my word on it. Scout's honor. Honest Injun. I pledge allegiance to the flag

I used to be in the Army, as a trombone player. But I didn't like the Army, so I got out and came home. Which of course went over really well at home. Now I sleep all day, go to the gym in the evening, and at night I go to bars and hustle pool for money. When I come home at three or four in the morning, as I open the gate to the short gravel driveway that leads from the dead-end circle to my parents' small old white (painted) brick house, I say "White Fang doggie" to the wagging dancing canine. Each night I tell myself that I must get back to writing, that the following evening I will stay home and get back to work, but of course it does not turn out that way.

On the way to the concert:
We saw a house covered with Christmas lights. "You could say they're decorated," my diminutive friend said. (He is small, even for his age.)
"Just a little bit," I returned. "That probably took a few minutes to do."
"Just a few," he said.

"Actually, they probably have a little box with a button on it that holds all the lights, and all they do to put them out is push the button and it shoots them out and they're there. Probably takes about five seconds."

"Yeah, right."

"And then when they get ready to take them down, they just push the other button—whoosh!—and all the lights fly back into the box. Five seconds tops."

"Yeah, right." He seems amused.

So then I ask him if he remembers, when he was in the sixth grade, what I told him I would do if he didn't practice.

"You mean the button on the wall and the alligator pit?"

"That's it."

"With all your other students that didn't practice. You told me that my *first* lesson."

"No, I didn't—not the first one."

"Yes you did—I'll never forget that." He is happy in remembering.

"So what did you think of me?"

"I thought, 'Man, this guy is weird.'" He laughs goofily.

"Well, you were right."

"Yep. Sure was."

On the way back from the concert:

"You know this is crazy, but I've been meaning to ask you this forever," he says a little uncertainly, naïvely. "Do you have a girl-friend?"

"No, I don't," I say. "I was dating Julia Roberts, but I had to let her go. She wouldn't give me any space."

"Julia Roberts. Yeah, right." He seems pleased with the answer.

So a couple days later my little friend's mother calls me at home. They're going to buy him a professional model trombone for Christmas, and they'd like my advice. So I tell her to get a Bach 42B.

"Okay, now, what about a Bolton? The man at the music store said they have a Bolton in stock. He said they were what a lot of people were going to now. What do you think of them?"

I explain to her that most professionals play Bachs. I also tell her about a mail-order company where she can get one about seven hundred dollars cheaper than from the music store. I give her the company's toll-free number.

"So Bach is the best?" she says. She is a very nice woman and has always been unusually cooperative, a great pleasure to deal with as far as parents go. I know she is only trying to do the right thing.

"Unless you get a Johnson. It's a custom horn that's just been out a few years, and they're really expensive. They start at two thousand. He wouldn't need one of those unless he plays professionally someday. Even then he wouldn't necessarily *need* it, lots of professionals—most, actually—still play on Bachs. I guess it's just a matter of how much dough you have to blow. I guess if I was rich I would buy the Johnson for my kid, which of course I don't have any kids (I'm not even married) and I'm not rich. Are you rich, Mrs. Bigbottom? Of course I guess a true parent would get the Johnson anyway, even if he (she) couldn't afford it, he'd find a way because he gave a damn about his kid. Do you give a damn about your kid, Mrs. Bigbottom? Because it really doesn't make a rat's ass to me one way or the other what you get the little snot. To tell you the truth, I get tired of fuckin' with the little shit because he doesn't practice half the shit I give him to work on. To tell you the truth I'd just as soon not have to teach the little bastard. I really don't give a damn what you—"

Click, I hear. She has hung up. I just lost the best student I ever taught.

So I'm at the Christmas Eve service at our Episcopal church, and people are giving me dirty looks, particularly the older people my parents' age. Like I've betrayed them or something. They always used to smile at me like I was something special, like I had potential.

So I'm waiting in line for communion, and I know it's supposed to be serious, but I can't help cracking a big grin. I've fought this impulse many times before in similar situations, and I always managed to keep it down. Not this time, though. There's no stopping it—an irresistible force.

It just so happens that the young girl (she looks to be about fifteen) standing directly in front of me in line is wearing a tight purple dress, and it just so happens that trying its best to escape from the dress is one of the nicest derrières I have ever witnessed. So naturally I just ease a step forward, right into the midst of that soft full roundness, and of course it's all downhill from there, readerwoe...

The State I Loved You In

A low sound in the hollows
fills low places, fills hollows,
carves a hollow from the right place
or hollows being in place,
a sound I heard
in a strange place,
in a strange state,
just off the road in southern Utah,
just over the border, just off the desert,
where a field of wheat ran gold
into the sun as if it were a bright day in February,
where a half-ring of black boulders rose by the road
where we stopped to let the children out,
where the boulders caught the sound, where we spilled
the coke we'd been tooting from Fresno and swore
that was it, we'd marry, knowing we were that far
from home. And where we relieved ourselves, our hollow promises,
and agreed to raise the children into the bourgeois names
of washed-up empire—Nicholas and Alexandra.
You shucked your promises with stalks of wheat
I said I'd carry as a bouquet, and all of us heard
that choir singing in the rocks, angels, we thought, sobbing,
or the tabernacle choir rehearsal gone astray and echoing
this far from home. The children were afraid
until you broke all your promises, which was your way,
as memory lasts longer than truth. I left
the fragile and golden wheat
on the dashboard of my old Alliance
when it was hauled to the junkyard in Spook Hollow,
shame of a name, outside the town where the wind
makes the small sound, a hollow sound, as of the sound
made by breath across empty gourds
or land

or the sound pulsing beneath a storm, beneath electrical wires,
beneath slabs of concrete lining front yards,
a sound just between stone and earth, like the low whistle
in the scar pockets the body
forms around foreign implants, the roar of insistent blood
the moment before we faint, which may be
what we hear before we die,
may be what you heard before you died,
still man, quiet man,
after you no longer heard
the voices that kept trying to call you back to the road.

Shadow

You came upon me like a shadow
and you came into me like a shadow
and there you dwelled within me
and I in you;
we were cast on the black water—
we were cast by the will of the wind—
and thrown upon the darker shore
where no things grow
and the dry leaves gather
and we cannot recognize
the forms of light.

Lintel

I stood before the lintel;
the door swung open then.
Your name was there, and mine,
and the date of every birth—
all was clear as day,
but they could not bring me in.
Beyond another door
and then another, endless
more, yet the distance had
been measured in the dust—
one print stepping after
another and none of them
turning back to us.

LOREN GRAHAM

The Banquet

I sat in a crowded place away from you
at dinner and did not pray you'd come near:
did not imagine the hall our private room;
did not want to approach you with an air
of feigned indifference, leaving my meal-
time companions behind; did not conspire
alone to lure you into talk, to feel
the air crackling between us, the desire
like some doomed insect trapped behind the blinds,
pent up and buzzing, helpless; did not think
how easy it would be to change our minds
and reconcile, laughing over a drink,
our arms just touching; did not make a wish
for you—no, never dreamed a word of this.

Ghazal

Last night I walked in a field. The moon
lit the snow: snow gray as the moon.

And tried to remember your face—Luna Moth,
circling the cold flame of the moon.

At the same moment you looked up, protracting
the old angle: self, secret-love, and the moon.

The earth was young too. But what's left to say
about youth? What hasn't been told to the moon?

One circles the other, swirling in a black pool.
Adiós, says the earth. *Adieu,* says the moon.

And like a child I think: How else would she follow me?
Whenever I turn: your face in the moon.

But love? Love is a coyote snarling your name,
gnawing its leg by the light of the moon.

Israel

He brought vanilla candles. Some gift. My mother squeezed them into old silver on the mantle and lit each one. They scorched the wall. Even our best sofas couldn't make up for the cheesy, rundown way the wall looked now. Still, this was London, not New York, and my mother didn't even seem to notice. She was on a date. Derek Duncalf, the anesthesiologist, wrapped his legs down around the last curve of the love seat. My mother bent over, pushed a log back inside the grate. I was saying hello.

"Hello, Dr. Duncalf."

My mother said that Derek Duncalf put his patients under by talking to them. But his tedious droning didn't cure him from occasionally leaping across all obstacles to pin my mother to the wall. My mother liked this. She enjoyed the telling of it. She giggled and described his whining and pleading. Their dance of love was set. She would never give in; he would sleep, then spring, then be rebuffed. He sent her flowers: huge sprays, branches hacked from trees in first budding, wired into fanciful shapes. They leaned against the empire mirror in the foyer, and my mother would sniff at them, then snore, then laugh.

We were waiting for my father. My father had a small bachelor flat not a block away from us on Upper Brook Street. Every day he would pass by on his way to the office, on his way home. Sometimes he would stop in for a drink. All his things were still with us, half-packed in bags, a favorite painting taken down from the wall, rehung, taken down. Six months of this, eight months, nine months. My mother began to date. My mother began to wear falls—hair attached from the crown of her head that ran down the length of her spine. She loved to wear hot pants and silk shirts and lace-up boots and false eyelashes and brown lipstick and no bra. And though I could see only her faults, the thickness of her upper arms, the glazed look in her encumbered eyes, men came regularly to her living room.

One day Derek brought a friend, Dr. Dan Ovita. Dr. Ovita was from Israel. My mother made a huge fire in the marble fireplace. The flames traced wild shadows on the silver of her caftan. My mother tossed her fall from right to left, and Dr. Dan Ovita studied her and me. He studied us both, and his gaze made us forget to look out the window at half past six to determine whether my father would be coming for cocktails that day. As it happened, he didn't, not that day, not the next.

Dr. Dan Ovita talked about the war in Israel. The war was fresh. The soldiers were young men and women not much older than me. They were fighting to keep their homeland. Dr. Dan Ovita was the most famous hand surgeon in Israel. He told us that hands were more fragile than butterflies, and when he was able to fix a mortified palm, it seemed a miracle, even to him.

I couldn't forget what he said about hands. My own hands were being leeched of their delicacy by the stones I was gaining. Stones. In London we weighed ourselves in stones—pounds were for money. No amount of dieting, and diet aids, and worse things—abrading my own throat—could help me. It didn't matter. I was getting bigger by the day. My breasts bloomed. But I saw them as two folds among many. By the time my father had been in his bachelor flat a full nine months, I was heavier by seven and a half stones, fifty-four pounds, a pound and a half for every week he had deserted us.

My mother explained: My father needed to forget. We reminded him of all the things he could no longer stand to think of. Without us to remind him, those bad memories shrank and disappeared. He forgot my baby brother's death, he forgot the false indictment, jail, he forgot betrayals and infidelities. He forgot the woman who wrote to my mother saying she'd kill herself, then did, falling from a second-story window. Not so far to fall, but still, she died. Without us, my father was beginning life all over again. He was brand-new, my mother said. He still missed us as people, though, and that's why he visited without calling first, as if he still lived with us. He used his own key, he showered and changed, he smoked and made phone calls. Each time, after he left, my mother found reason to hit me. Once she punched my right breast, and the sensation in that nipple flew away for good.

Dr. Dan Ovita told me that sometimes the men and women's hands he operated on blossomed like flowers. They became saturated with feeling. Patients took up painting who'd never noticed the color of anything before. People played piano and guitar and mandolins and their families felt haunted and grateful at the same time. One patient who could neither paint nor fathom a tune made hand-shadows on walls move like living things. Dr. Ovita was talking about physical therapy, not magic. There was nothing magical about Dr. Ovita, which was why I liked him. He never disappeared; he never changed shape.

One evening Derek Duncalf and Dr. Ovita drank grappa with my mother. They were celebrating because Dr. Ovita had convinced many surgeon-volunteers to go to Israel for three-month rotations. By the end of the week he'd be home setting up field hospitals on the borders. They all nibbled on tiny sandwiches I made of pressed-down brown bread and watercress. Their stomachs were barely lined by such things, and the grappa felled them each like a tree. Derek Duncalf's boneless legs rippled down to the floor, and I thought his shoe might catch fire, it was so close to the flames. But Dr. Dan Ovita repositioned Derek's body like a kindly choreographer might before melting himself into a graceful puddle on the carpet. My mother's head flipped to the left, one of her breasts scrubbed against her blouse. Under brown silk the nipple looked gnarly and rough, something to scour a pot. That scared me. I couldn't help but run my tongue over my inner cheeks, though she'd never nursed me. Then I went to bed.

Even I was asleep when my father came the next morning to find his blue tie. But I heard him weeping, as I had so often in my dreams. My father's crying sounded like the most deserted baby's, a howling, choking wail. I found him on the side of the bathtub holding his blue tie. He said he didn't understand. He just didn't understand. I felt afraid to touch him. His mouth looked swollen.

"Daddy."

"Don't," he said.

The only things I could think to say were old things, good things. More things he couldn't stand us for. Especially me. I remembered everything.

I went to find my mother. The curtains were only half-pulled in the master bedroom. Light slipped in from the courtyard. My mother was still semi-dressed. Hot pants crinkled, wedged at the tops of her thighs, stockings all snagged. Her fall lay at the foot of the bed like a dead dog. Derek Duncalf was stripped completely, and his body had little contour, just flesh and hair and a short stub of a penis I could barely stand to look at. He smelled like smoked salmon. I had to stop breathing when I leaned across him to shake my mother. She sat up, and her breasts fell into order, the nipples perfect. My father's sobs from the bathroom pulled her toward him, just as she was, like a sleepwalker.

Her hair sprouted in tufts around her face. She pulled my father's fingers from his eyes. His hands were the best part of him. She held them like eggs, very still between her own. My father's face smoothed to a wet red calmness. My mother called him sweet George over and over, which is not his name, not a name I'd ever heard before. Their foreheads touched—she leaning in from her seat on the bidet, he from the lip of the tub. Their bodies made an imperfect arch. I backed out, feeling nauseous, the nausea my mother might have felt when first carrying me. I passed my own bathroom with the green ivy paper climbing to the ceiling, all the way up and across the ceiling, and I passed on the opportunity to suffer my own hand reaching into my throat. I dressed for school. On the way out I wrote a brief note and stuffed it into the pocket of the folded, sleeping Dr. Ovita. "I'm coming with you," I wrote.

And Dr. Ovita agreed. My parents said okay, I could go to school in Israel, learn another language. But school is not a big deal to me. In summers I help pitch tents for the surgeons, and I am never afraid. In winter I come to this kibbutz, where I am famous for my cooking and have a soldier-lover with hands that feel like tiny rabbits hopping all over me while I laugh. My hair is very long. I wear a bra as soft as a blanket. My lover speaks to my breast in Hebrew. His guttural sound will surely raise it from the dead. And when I write my parents, my father signs each reply: Our love.

Seen

In your field of vision, there is a place where no image is fixed.
It is a place where injury carved its cave of nothing,
gathered blackness around a splinter's wooden slip.
One eye, you say, looks inward
while the other scans the world. One eye
examines the self's invisible wanting.
In that equation, I believe myself to be
a point connecting one place to another,
somewhere you paused to draw lines to the next warm station.
I emit no light, no heat
but gather, in cupped hands, what fell to the ground
when limbs were shaken by your copper wind.

An Awful Story

When she came into his room he was asleep
and when she touched him, he woke—
her hand on his shoulder, her knee at his mouth,
and in the darkness, she looked like a boy.

When he tried to sit up she covered his ears
with her hands: "Save ourselves from ourselves,"
she said, and then a wind stirred in the room
as if she'd placed those words in his mouth.

The Blame

That which you made me do I did.
That which you made me say I said.
Now the blame, like oil over water,
spreads, and so our life together
that began in vows—the licensed oath—
has leased itself back to us both:
what we knew and couldn't know
what our words no longer show.

VIRGIL SUAREZ

In the House of White Light

When my grandmother left the house
        to live with my aunts, my grandfather,

who spent so much time in the sugar
        cane fields, returned daily to the emptiness

of the clapboard house he built
        with his own hands, and he sat in the dark

to eat beans he cooked right in the can.
        There in the half-light he thought of all he'd lost,

including family, country, land, sometimes
        he slept upright on that same chair,

only stirred awake by the restlessness
        of his horse. One night during a lightning

storm, my grandfather stripped naked
        and walked out into the fields around

the house saying *"Que me parta un rayo,"*
        May lightning strike me, and he stood

with his arms out, the hard rain pelted
        his face, and then the lightning fell

about him, and he danced and cradled
        lightning bolts in his arms, but they

kept falling, these flashes of white light,
        and he ran back inside and brought out

an armful of large mason jars my grandmother
                used for pickling, and he filled them

with fractal light. Like babies, he carried
                the jars inside and set them all about the house,

and the house filled with the immense
                blinding light that swallowed everything

including the memories of how each nail
                sunk into the wood, the water level rose

in the well, the loss of this country,
                the family who refused to accept him now,

that in this perpetual waking, the world
                belonged to those who believed in the power

of electricity, those moments zapped
                of anguish, isolation, this clean and pure

act of snatching lightning out of heavy air,
                plucking lightning like flowers from a hillside.

DINAH BERLAND

A Walk at Dusk

after a painting by Caspar David Friedrich (1774–1840)

Come with me, toward the leafless trees. See
the way they lean, dazed with fog and grief
as they seek out one another in the haze?
Isn't that how we are able to go on—by believing
all that matters will one day be revealed?
That is why I made the waxing moon so sharp,
its violet face aglow, why I put the moon under
the influence of Venus, though we know
these lovers are light years from each other.
But I have not brought you here to talk about
astronomy or painterly technique but rather
magnetism of a different order. Over there—
now you see it: the megalithic tomb.
See how that massive rock appears to float
like a ship asunder? This weighty sepulcher
will not leave me alone. I have painted it
under a hood of snow, girdled it in broken oaks,
glazed it with opaque aspersions. Some evenings,
walking here alone, I am that rock—or I am
a man trapped beneath its lid, dense
with melancholia, my fur hat a granite wheel,
my stained hands sunk deep into the pockets
of my cape. I have heard it said that memory
is a form of recovery, a healing. But sometimes
when I venture to this field at the dislocating
hour—the very hour that slips across
our foreheads at this moment, before
the earth rolls over in the star-cast void
like a capsized ship and all of us gone with it—
memory breaches the grave. Walk with me
awhile, I pray you. I am drowning on dry land,
and only a stranger's gaze can save me.

JOHN BENSKO

The Hidden Street

The dogs have stopped barking. Even the grass
has grown quieter, holding back from the wind.
As you and I walk down the sidewalk, our voices
are like a memory, whose deep
purpose has gone inside, into the walls
and floors and ceilings, where it no longer
reaches the air but lies in wait for us.

Where did we take the wrong turn? Some might
say it was right, onto this street
of Victorian houses, with their cupolas
of children looking down, and owners
sweeping their wide porches, as if the dust
they raise were sound, and the faces
pressed against glass were not boredom

but the shouts of afternoon games.
Have you and I become hawks
sweeping forceful pinions above
the dim unsuspecting? Or are we moths
attracted to windows, while preferring
the dark corner and the night?
The street has no answer. Its voice

is victim, is night. It is the hidden
street we walk down afternoons
surprised to find it once more, to recognize
its antique beauty, its deadly silence.

Black Elvis

At five p.m. precisely, Black Elvis began to get ready. First, he laid out his clothes, the dark suit, the white dress shirt, the two-tone oxfords. In the bathroom, he used a depilatory powder to remove the stubble from his face, then carefully brushed his teeth and gargled with Lavoris. He applied a light coating of makeup, used a liner to deepen the effect of his eyes. They were big eyes, the color of old ivory, and examining them in the mirror, he had to remind himself once again whose they were.

At the bus stop, his guitar precariously stowed in a chipboard case held together by a bungee cord, he was watched by two shirt-less boys on a stoop, drinking sodas. Their young, dark torsos emerged out of enormous dungarees like shoots sprouting.

"Yo," one of them called. "Let me see that."

Black Elvis stayed where he was, but tightened his grip on the case. The boys stood and walked over to him. The sun hung low in the sky, turning the fronts of the rowhouses golden red.

"Are you a Muslim, brother?" asked the smaller of the two. His hair was cornrowed, and one eye peered unnaturally to the side.

Black Elvis shook his head. He wondered how hot it still was. Eighty, at least.

"He's a preacher," said the other one. "Look at him." This boy, though larger, gave the impression of being less sure of himself. His sneakers were untied and looked expensive and new.

"Singing for Jesus, is that right?"

"No," said Black Elvis.

"For who, then?" said the smaller one.

"For an audience, my man. I have a gig." He knew this boy. Sometimes he drew pictures on the sidewalk with colored chalk.

"Yeah?" The boy trained his one useful eye on the guitar case, the other apparently examining something three feet to the left. "Go on and play something, then."

"I'm a professional. No professional going to play songs at no bus stop."

"When the bus come?"

Black Elvis examined his watch. "Anytime now."

"You got time. Play us something."

"Was I talking to this here lamppost? Black Elvis don't play no bus stops."

"Black *what*?" said the bigger of the two boys.

"Elvis."

"Dude is tripping *out*."

"Yo, Black Elvis. Why don't you help us out with a couple of dollars? Me and my boy here, we need to get some things at the store."

He considered. He had bus fare and another eight dollars on top of that, which he intended to use for beer at Slab's. In case of emergency, there was the ten-dollar bill in his shoe, under the Air-Pillo Insole. He dug into his pocket and pulled out two ones.

"All right, then," he said, and handed them the money.

The smaller one leaned very close as he took it. He was about the same size as Black Elvis, and he smelled strongly of underarm.

"You crazier than shit, ain't you?"

"You take that two dollars," Black Elvis said calmly as the bus pulled in, "go on over to Kroger's, and get yourself some Right Guard."

At Slab's, the smell of grilled meat permeated the walls and the painted windows that advertised ribs, beer, and live music, and extended well out into the parking lot. The dinner rush had already started, and there was a good-sized line of people waiting to place orders. Larry was working the register, grizzled white stubble standing out against his nut-brown skin, grease flames shooting up from the grill behind him as slabs and half slabs were tossed onto the fire. If hell had a front desk, he looked like he was manning it.

Butch, who ran the blues jam, was at his usual front table near the stage, finishing a plate of ribs, beans, and slaw. "Black Elvis," he said, with enthusiasm. He wiped his mouth with a napkin, then smoothed his goatee. His pink face glistened with a thin layer of sweat. "What is up?"

"Oh, you know, same old, same old. You got me?"

"I got you, man, don't worry." He tapped a legal pad with one thick finger. "Wouldn't be the blues jam without Black Elvis."

"I know that's right."

"You heard about Juanita?"

"No."

"Oh, man. She died last night. In her sleep. Put in her regular shift, just sassing people like she always did, you know. Didn't seem like anything was wrong with her at all. But I guess she had a bad ticker. She was a little overweight."

"She was, at that." He thought about Juanita's huge butt and breasts, how she more waddled than walked. But dead? How could that be?

"Yeah, it's a sad thing," said Butch. "Kind of makes you realize how fragile it all is, for all of us."

He watched as the drummer hauled the house snare drum out from the women's bathroom, where it was stored, up next to the stage. The wall behind the stage was painted to look like Stone Mountain, but instead of Confederate generals, the faces looking down at the crowd were those of B. B. King, Muddy Waters, Robert Johnson, and someone else who Black Elvis could never be quite sure about. Whoever had done the painting wasn't much of an artist.

"Hey, you want a beer?" Butch poured the remainder of the pitcher on the table into what looked like a used glass. "Go on, man, on the house."

Black Elvis picked up a napkin and ran it carefully around the rim of the glass. "Thanks," he said.

He found himself a seat next to a table of rich white folks who had been to some movie and were arguing about whether the actress in it had had her breasts enlarged. It had been a long time since Black Elvis had been to the movies, although he sometimes watched the ones they had running back in the video department of the Kroger's where he cut meat. They mostly looked the same to him, flickering postage stamps of color. They ought never to have gone to color, he thought. A picture ought to be in black and white. He remembered going to a picture with his father years ago that had pirates in it and Errol Flynn. His father wouldn't buy him popcorn, said it was a waste of money. He must have been about eight. The war was over. There were ships and sword fighting and men with long hair, and suddenly his daddy was pressing a hard-boiled egg into his hand and saying, "Go on, boy, take it."

He ate the egg, shucking it carefully into his hand and placing the shells into the pocket of his shirt, while all around him he smelled the popcorn he really wanted.

He looked up. They'd asked him something, but he could not be sure what.

"Napkins?"

He pushed the dispenser toward them. He'd drifted someplace, it seemed. He took a swallow of beer. He needed something inside him, that was all—some weight to keep him from floating away. He was Black Elvis. He had a show to put on.

He'd been doing the jam now for four years. Everyone knew him. They relied on him. Sometimes he changed his repertoire around a little bit, threw in "I Can't Help Falling in Love" or something else unusual—he had a version of "You Were Always on My Mind," but it just never sounded right to him—but for the most part he was a Sun Sessions man. "That's All Right" for an opener. "Hound Dog." "All Shook Up." "Milkcow Blues." If there was a band, he'd play with them—he liked that—but it didn't matter, he could do his songs by himself, too. He twisted his lip, stuck out his hip, winked at the ladies. Two years ago, the *Creative Loafing* had done an article on Slabs, and his picture appeared next to it, almost as if his face were an addition to the mural, and he kept this taped to the wall next to his bed.

There were moments he'd tucked away in his mind the way people keep photos in their wallets, ones that stood out from the succession of nights of cigarette and pork-grease smell, of cold beers and loud music. The time he'd explained to a fine young blond-haired girl, whose boyfriend had come down to show off his rock and roll guitar playing, that it was Elvis who had said, "I'd rather see you dead, little girl, than to be with another man," in "Baby, Let's Play House," and not the Beatles, and the way she'd looked at him then and said, "You mean they *stole* it?" and he smiled and said, "That's exactly what I mean." Or the time a young white man in a suit gave him a fifty-dollar tip and said, "You're the best dang thing I've seen in this whole dang town, and I been here one year exactly come Friday."

He should have been the first one called. That was usual. That was the way things went on blues jam night. But that wasn't what happened. Instead, Butch played a few songs to open—"Let the Good Times Roll" and "Messin' with the Kid"—then stepped to the microphone and looked right past Black Elvis.

"We got a real treat here tonight," he said. "Let's all give it up for Mr. Robert Johnson. I'm serious now, that's his real name. Give him a nice hand."

From somewhere in the back, a person in an old-fashioned-looking suit and fedora worked his way up through the crowded restaurant, holding a black guitar case up high in front of him. Trailing out from the back of the hat was a straight black ponytail. When he reached the stage he opened the case and took out an antique guitar. He turned around and settled into a chair, pulling the boom mike down and into place for him to sing, while Butch arranged another mike for the instrument. Black Elvis just stared.

The man was Chinese.

"Glad to be here," said Robert Johnson. "I only been in Atlanta a week, but I can tell I'm going to like it a lot already." He grinned a big, friendly grin. His voice sounded Southern. "Just moved here from Memphis," he said. "First thing I did, I said, 'Man, where am I gonna get me some decent ribs in this town?'" He plucked at the guitar, made a kind of waterfall of notes tumble out of it. "I can tell I'm going to be putting on some weight around here." There was laughter from the crowd.

Black Elvis drank some more beer and listened carefully as Robert Johnson began to play the Delta blues. He was good, this boy. Probably spent years listening to the original recordings, working them out note for note. Either that, or he had a book. Some of those books had it like that, exact translations. But that wasn't important. What was important was on the *inside*. You had to *feel* the music. That just didn't seem likely with a Chinese man, even one that came from Memphis.

He did "Terraplane Blues." He did "Sweet Home Chicago" and "Stones in My Pathway." He played "Love in Vain." Black Elvis felt something dark and opiate creeping through his blood, turning harder and colder as it did so. On the one hand, it should have been him up there, making the crowd love him. But the more he watched, the more he was convinced that he simply could not go on after Robert Johnson. With his pawn shop guitar and clumsy playing, he'd just look like a fool.

He watched Butch's face and saw the enjoyment there. He'd never seen the crowd at Slab's be so quiet or attentive to a performer. Robert Johnson *did* feel the music, even if he was Chinese. It was strange. Black Elvis glanced toward the front door and wondered if there were any way at all he might slip unnoticed through the crowded tables and out.

When Robert Johnson finished his set, people applauded for what seemed like hours. He stood and bowed, antique guitar tucked under one arm. Black Elvis felt he was watching the future, and it was one that did not include him. But that was negative thinking. You couldn't let yourself fall into that. He'd seen it happen to other people his age, the shadows who walked around his neighborhood, vacant-eyed, waiting to die. Esther, who lived in 2-C, just below him, who watched television with the volume all the way up and only opened the door once a week for the woman from Catholic Social Services to come deliver her groceries. That woman had stopped up to see Black Elvis, but he'd sent her away. Ain't no Catholic, he'd said. That's not really necessary, she told him. So he told her he carried his own groceries, and got a discount on them, too. And as she was leaving he asked her if she knew what God was, and when she didn't answer, he told her: "The invention of an animal that knows he's going to die."

They were talking to him again, those people at the next table. He shook his head and wondered where he'd gone. His mind was like a bird these days.

"You're up," they told him. "They want you."

He brought his guitar up onto the stage. Robert Johnson had taken a seat with Butch, and they were talking intently about something. Butch had out a datebook and was writing in it. Butch also booked the music for Slab's on the other nights, the ones where the performers got paid. Robert Johnson's Chinese eyes squinted tight as pistachio nuts when he smiled.

"Black Elvis," someone shouted. He heard laughter.

"I'm going to do something a little different," he said into the microphone. "A good person passed last night. Some of you probably heard about it by now. Juanita—" He struggled to find her last name, then heard himself say "Williams," which he was certain was wrong, but was the only name he could come up with. "Juanita was, you know, family for us here at Slab's, and we loved her. So I'd like to dedicate this song to Juanita. This one for you, baby."

He played a chord and was not surprised when his fourth string snapped like an angry snake striking. Ignoring this, he began to sing.

"Amazing grace, how sweet the sound . . ."

He didn't know if the next chord should be the same, or different, so he just played E again. It wasn't right, but it wasn't that wrong.

"That saved a wretch like me . . ."

He remembered his mother singing this. He could see her on the porch, stroking his sister Mae's head, sitting in the red metal chair with the flaking paint, the smell of chicken cooking in the kitchen flowing out through the patched window screen. His own voice sounded to him like something he was hearing at a great distance.

"I once was lost, but now I'm found . . ."

The people were staring at him. Even Larry had stopped ringing up sales and was watching, the fires continuing to dance behind him.

"Was blind, but now I see."

He lowered his head and hit a few more chords. He felt like he was in church, leading a congregation. He looked up, then nodded somberly and went back to his chair.

"That was beautiful, man," said Butch, coming over to him. "Just fucking beautiful."

Robert Johnson offered to buy him a beer.

"All right," said Black Elvis. "Molson's."

"Molson's, it is." He was gone a few minutes, then returned with a pitcher and two glasses. "I like a beer with flavor," he said. "Microbrews and such."

"I like beer that's cold," said Black Elvis. "I like it even better if it's free."

"Hard to argue with that, my man." He filled the glasses. "I'm sorry to hear about your friend."

Black Elvis stared at him.

"Juanita?"

"That's right. Tragedy. They say she had a bad ticker. She *was* a little overweight, now." He thought again about her. She'd had a lot of facial hair, he remembered that. And she used to wear this chef's hat.

"This is a nice place," said Robert Johnson, looking around. The next group was setting up on stage. "Real homey."

"This is the best place for ribs and blues in Atlanta. Don't let no one tell you different." He peered at Robert Johnson's round, white face. "So, you from Memphis, huh?"

"That's right."

"Memphis, China?"

Robert Johnson laughed. "I'm Korean, not Chinese. Well, my parents are. I was born here. But I've always loved black music. I grew up around it, you know."

"What kind of guitar that is you play?"

"Martin. 1924 00-28 Herringbone. I wish I could tell you I found it in an attic or something, but it's not that good a story. I paid a lot for it. But it's got a nice sound, and it fits with the whole Robert Johnson act, you know?" He adjusted his tie. "I've learned that it's not enough to just be good at what you do, you have to have a marketing angle, too."

"Marketing, you say."

"I've got me a gig here already for next weekend."

He was quiet for a moment. "You been to Graceland?"

"Graceland! Well, of course I've been to Graceland. Everyone in Memphis has been to Graceland."

"What's it like?"

"What's it like?" He gave a silver ring on his middle finger a half turn. "Tacky. In some ways, it feels like holy ground, but at the same time, you also feel like you're at an amusement park. The Jungle Room is pretty cool, I guess."

"Sun Studios?"

"They have tours, but I've never done one. If you're so interested, you ought to go."

"You think so?"

"Sure. Why not?"

"You got connections there? Like who could get me a gig?"

Robert Johnson considered this. Black Elvis realized that he'd done exactly what he'd wanted not to do, which was to put this person in a position where he had power over him. But he couldn't get it out of his head that there was something about this meeting that was more than chance. He had a feeling Robert Johnson was someone he was *supposed* to meet, if only he could determine why.

"I don't think so. I mean, if you're going to do an Elvis thing, you're probably better off just about anyplace *but* Memphis. Of course, that's just my opinion."

"I'll bet they don't have no black Elvises."

"Are you kidding? Black, Chinese, Irish, Jewish, you name it. You think fat white men in hairpieces have the market cornered on Elvis impersonation? I know a place where they have a dwarf who sings 'Battle Hymn of the Republic' every evening at ten while two strippers give each other a bath, right onstage."

For a moment, he imagined a big stage—an opera house—with hundreds of Elvises of all shapes and colors pushing and shoving each other to get to the front. The thought made him shiver. "Don't matter. I'm an original."

"No doubt. If you don't mind my asking, what made you decide to start doing this?" He looked at Black Elvis with admiration. "I love your hair, incidentally. I mean, if I looked like you, Jesus. I'd be working all the time. You just have that natural blues man look. You could be John Lee Hooker's cousin or something."

"I don't care much for blues music," said Black Elvis. He sniffed. "Never have."

"Really?"

"I like that rock and roll."

"Well, whatever makes you happy." Robert Johnson made a move to get up.

"No, wait," said Black Elvis, suddenly anxious. "Tell me something. Is that what you think? Have I gotten it wrong all this time? Should I be doing something else? You play good, you sing good, you know about marketing. Just tell me, and I'll listen. I don't have that much time left."

Robert Johnson stood up and adjusted his fedora. He looked slightly embarrassed. "I gotta go talk to a young woman over there," he said. "She's been staring at me ever since I got here. I'm sure you understand." He picked up a napkin and held it out. "You got a little nosebleed going."

Black Elvis took the napkin and held it tight against his nose.

* * *

When he got home, Juanita was waiting for him in the living room, wearing her chef's hat and a stained serving apron, her wide body taking up half the sofa.

"You late," she said. "Did you have a good time?"

"Good time?" he said. He thought about this. He didn't really go to the blues jam for a good time. He went because it gave him a purpose, a place to be, and because by now it just seemed that if he *didn't* go, all hell might break loose. The sun might not come up in the morning. "I sang you a song," he said.

"That right? What you sing? One of them Elvis songs?"

" 'Amazing Grace.' "

"Well, that's nice. You've got blood on your shirt, you know."

"Mmmm-hmmmm." He pulled up a chair and sat opposite her. He had not turned on any lights, and her figure was shadowy and evanescent, like a glimpse of a fish below the surface of a fast stream. "You supposed to be dead, now."

"Supposed to be."

"Bad ticker, huh?"

"Just stopped on me."

"Hurt?"

"Shit yes. For a second it felt like someone hit me in the chest with a sledgehammer. Now, tell me the truth, how come you singing songs for me? You know I don't care for you much at all. I'd have thought the feeling was mutual."

"Let me turn on a light."

"Don't do that. I like it better in the dark. Come on, now, what's with the song?"

Black Elvis closed his eyes for a moment. "There was a man there, a Chinese man. He took my spot."

"And so you go all churchy? You just nothing but a hypocrite. Just a big old faker."

"I don't believe in you," said Black Elvis. "And I'm turning on the light."

"I don't believe in you, either," said Juanita. "Go ahead."

He cut on the light, and she was gone, as he'd suspected she would be. From the street below, he heard shouting and laughter. He went over to the window and pulled back the curtains just far enough to see.

The two boys he'd seen earlier were out in the middle of the street. One had a spray can of paint and was walking slowly back and forth, while the other, the bigger one, watched and occasionally shouted encouragement. At first, he couldn't tell what the image was, but then the lines began to come together and he realized that it was him the boy was painting, Black Elvis, spray-painted twenty feet high down the center of the street. He watched in amazement as the details took shape, his pompadour, the serious eyes, sideburns, pouting lips.

"Believe in me," he said. "Stupid woman."

Approaching 40

I never thought we'd meet. Now here he is,
swinging his arms like a speed-walker.

I thought he'd look ancient—almost half
a century—but in my telescope, he looks a lot

like me: a few less hairs, a limp I don't like
the look of, but not an old man, certainly,

though reading glasses dangle from his neck.
(Like those I saw Thursday, but refused

to buy.) No one but me would think him
scary, his sweatshirt a football jersey

with 40 on the front and back. (Don't ask me
how I see the back.) I know I should

stride up to meet him like a man. Instead,
I back away—or try. There's a glass wall

behind me, and a steel one behind him.
It's like a vice is squeezing us together.

I can't see through his wall, but I know
one thing that's on the other side—

and not as far ahead as my birth
lies behind. That thought stops me dead

in my tracks. The glass plate thumps me
two steps forward. 40 slows

as I speed up, but keeps coming.
If he's like past birthdays, I'll clasp him

when we meet—my long-lost twin—
and he'll evaporate. I'll feel a chill,

a sudden sweat, faintness, a just perceptible
pat on my back. Then, with luck,

I'll see a new speck in the distance:
41: walking steadily toward me.

Puritan Impulse

I talk the least
of what I covet
most, seldom look
at what I wish to see,
turn my nose away
from what smells best,
refuse to listen
to my favorite opera,
La Traviata,
even when it's sung
in town for free.
The Van Gogh show
can't make me walk
the block to view it,
no chef can intuit
what I might want,
and handing me jars
of caviar while
popping Veuve Cliquot
is not what I call love.

The rain last night
froze on the birches,
and today they bend
almost to breaking.
The sun makes every
branch distinct, too bright
to look at for long.
And that's excuse

enough for me
to look back down
to the road
I walk on, ice
on the pavement
so clear it's blue.

ANDREW ZAWACKI

Self-Portrait

Only the colorless eye is undistracted: a lake
Rubbed blue by twilight is not blue to the eye cast blue
And a violet sunset cannot be refracted
Violet through the violet eye. A crimson retina
Won't conceive the paint of a rigging blooded by dusk
Or the stain a star makes, cutting its patina
Crimson across a backwind disturbing the houseboat.

An idol requiring concealment, the eye is hewn
Without discernible hue, conferring the spectrum it lacks:
Eviscerated axiom of presence, the eye is a naught
Diffracting weather and water, and exits itself for the sake
Of what it reveals: a condition of vantage, a contract
With the mooring ropes and canvas it perceives,
Cataract the extracted vanishing point.

The pupil is polished black as the hull of a yacht
So the eye won't recognize darkness, only the fact
Of its coming on: a knot of isinglass that reflects
Lightning tracing paraphs around the harbor, it receives
Faint shadows enshrouding the dock, and orders by its law.
Not as judge but witness, emptying act for clarity
Yet inverting marina and watchman, as if to deceive:

Surface uncracked, improved upon, the eye is nothing it saw.

The Attic

It's September: I've moved into town,
into the attic of an old barn—a big open room I reach
by climbing a ladder that rises through a hole in the floor.
The room is long and high, with windows at each end,
a row of skylights that leak rain, and shake
and chatter in the northeast winds. I sleep beneath
the roof's steep pitch, my mattress flat on the boards,
looking up at the high ceiling where morning
diffuses downward in grains of bright dust.

This was the old painter's studio.
The light in those famous canvases is still here
—he couldn't carry it away with him—
though his paintings took away everything else,
opening space with a stroke of blue or yellow.
I think of his violent loves, the stories
they still tell about him here.
But how quiet and alive his paintings were,
how they quiver with life not yet realized.

The town is quiet in September.
Sometimes I hear people talking in the street.
Last night someone said they were going to wait for Michael,
and a voice said that Michael had gone home.
I walk the narrow path down to the marsh.
Wind hard in the dunes. Rain as I'm returning,
cutting through twisting streets, past gardens bent
low with rain, their colors a wash of gold.
I feel the air surround my body, feel it move
between my legs and between each finger.
as I walk, not mastering space, but in it.

And when the clouds open, the sky
so suddenly wide and high, no roof of leaves,
it seems there's nowhere to go but into sky or water.
I climb the narrow stairs that keep turning,
twisting inward, containing me, until they meet
the ceiling, which opens and I rise through the floor,
released into an openness I never learn to expect.

At the yellow table I sit and read
an interview with Picasso's lover, Françoise Gilot,
the only one to leave him and have another life.
She says she was not destroyed by him, as the others were:
"Because I am of the stuff that cannot be destroyed."
I felt something blow through me then.
Some devouring wind. Surely, then,
I am of the stuff that can be destroyed.
Haven't I felt it? The breaking of all I was?
Don't I sit and count my losses,
here in this room where all the life I knew has ended,
so bare with desire I seem to be eating sky?

That's how it is here: I'm lonely, sad;
the wind blows across the roof and I can't sleep.
Rain runs down the walls and drips into buckets
and runs along the floor, making dirty puddles on the boards.
A yellow table and a cupboard painted blue,
three chairs that don't match, or even balance rightly,
a dented bucket, its metal reflecting darkly
what is, what cannot be taken away.
These cracks in the boards reflecting light,
the stained sink and scarred counters luminous,
each object standing apart from the air,
to reveal a color deeper than color has ever been.
What's beautiful here? The whole thing
is beauty, a clarity not in things
but around them, complete.

And still I seem to remain, somehow, myself,
to remain at least something, at a loss

to know how much can be taken from me
and leave me only changed, not ruined,
alert in an emptiness so alive,
I recognize it as my life. What would be left,
the shape of it, then, this life? I said some beauty,
or radiance, an endless space I fall into,
or am taken up by, a brightness that holds me,
gathers life in the center of empty space,
like the vision of a life I have not lived.

JANE SHORE

Driving Lesson

"Name the eight states that begin with the letter *M*,"
Mohammed, my driving teacher, says.
I'm forty-one. Am I in school?
I glance at the rearview mirror, glad I can't see
my embarrassing STUDENT DRIVER bumper sticker.
I spread a ghost-map across the windshield,
quickly scroll down the East Coast, top to bottom.
"Maine. Massachusetts. Maryland."
Sweaty left hand gripping the turn signal,
I step on the gas, edging out
into congested Nassau Street in Princeton.

Twenty years since I last drove a car,
twenty years since I was a passenger in the red VW bug
my boyfriend Jeremy totaled on a Vermont back road,
twenty years since plastic surgery
fixed my broken cheekbone and eye socket,
my double vision, but not my fear.

"Are you hurt?" the priest had asked,
standing over us as we lay dazed
on bloody gravel, waiting for the ambulance.
Last rites? He'd just happened to be driving by.
Where am I? It's as if I just woke up
and found myself in the driver's seat, steering
the company car onto suburban country roads
past ugly half-built multimillion-dollar mansions,
muddy subdivisions, my right foot
on the gas, my cold hands on the wheel
nailed at ten and two o'clock.

"Minnesota," I say, "and Michigan,"
stopping inches from the crosswalk.
An orange hand flashed DON'T DON'T DON'T.
I check speedometer, fuel gauge—
the dashboard lit up like a cockpit.
"Mississippi, Missouri. Mobile, as in mobile,
as in auto*mobile*," I say. "Get it?"
Bearded Mohammed frowns, not in a joking mood.
Strip malls and luxury townhouse condos streak by
as his sneakers tap-dance around his safety brake.
We lurch. Stall. Cars behind us honk.
"Montana. Have I named them all?"

"Next lesson, I'll teach you how to park,"
Mohammed grins, adjusting his turban.
"Now, name four states that begin with the letter *A*."
I rev my engine. "Alabama, Arkansas."
At sea, I'm seasick in the Bible Belt.
"Arizona. Oh God, I almost forgot Alaska!"
"Relax," Mohammed says. "It's like I told you.
While you drive, you can keep your mind on
more than one thing at a time."

December 25

Christmas defeated Chanukah
once again last night
by a margin of three billion dollars
or so, but every time I hear
a Yiddish word like *bupkes*
in a movie (*L.A. Confidential*)
or when Oleg Cassini in that new play *Jackie*
calls a garment a *shmatta,* it's "good
for the Jews," as our parents used to say.
Meanwhile some things have
stayed the same; the drunken lout
in the street is still somebody's father.
Hey, kid, how does it feel to have a pop
that's a flop? And we had such good ideas
for changing the mental universe, if only
as a project in philosophy class, the one
I still dream about failing when I have
that dream everybody has, of being back
in college and needing this one course
to graduate, which I forgot to attend

BETHALEE JONES

Resurrection

Kneeling last night as children sometimes do,
After scrubbing off the filth of the day,
Undressed at my bed I bent and prayed
For some warm dream, for some comforting sooth
To say, *In the morning, arise.*

My sleep was elusive, as it often can be,
The starry firmament of self reproach
Circumnavigating this shabby host,
Beyond my control, refusing to heed
My carefully measured breath.

Sometime in the course, I gave up, gave in,
And night flashed his whip, drove his black horse,
Charged in a dust-raising run, making short
Work of my shoddy framework of sin.
Then Dream's scrim descended.

I was sitting at dusk revering my hands,
Sad because they were separate from me,
They held the promise, while I held the key,
When miraculously I clasped them hand in hand.
And this morning I arose again.

The Mourning Party

To an outsider, the grieving at the Burns Bungalows looked like revels. Mrs. Oates, the registered guest, counted five men climbing the hill to the main office with six-packs of beer in each hand. Women came, too, bearing plates covered with dishtowels, babies, or crock pots in their arms, or long bottles wrapped in paper bags. Mrs. Oates turned back the old curtain on her unit and watched them arrive—the inhabitants. Some looked like fishermen, young whiskered boys with honest eyes, sinewy from their struggles on the ocean. In the yard, a police official climbed out of a marked car. He hitched his pants to the lip of his belly, then opened the rear door to the poke and brought out a flowered casserole.

Two young women who'd borne the dead man babies still lived here, fanning flames. Over cocktails in the office the night before, they'd told her stories: Becky and Melody were the names. *Look at us,* they kept saying as they spun out episodes, as if they couldn't see themselves and thought that she might see something. Becky urged Mrs. Oates to join the mourning party. "You seem like real people!" Becky said.

Why not? thought Mrs. Oates. She was drawn to human interest—and all the talk was rich. Without looking, she ran red lipstick over her mouth. Then the curtain swung down over the rotten jamb, and Mrs. Oates appeared in the dirt yard with a package of corn nuts and the remains of her bottle of rye to chip in.

Buck Burns was the dead man's name; his mother and father ran the Bungalows and were the hosts of the party. While mourners walked up the hill from town and Mrs. Oates walked down from her bungalow, Mrs. Burns stood in the kitchenette of the front office among bowls of ambrosia. She wore her black hair like a hat, piled and sprayed into a nest. She wore tight slacks and a sweater, and two strings of pearls around her neck a Boston man had used one time to pay his bill. A plate of cream cheese and cherry sandwiches lay broken on the floor in front of her, and the pink triangles looked abused. Buck's dog lay mangy on the linoleum, gnawing on an old deer bone. When Mrs. Burns bent over to pick lint from her slacks, the dog jumped up and wrapped its forelegs around her, drooling from its black lips.

"Git on!" she told it. She shifted her cigarette to the other corner of her mouth and kicked the dog out of her way. "Git on!"

Mr. Burns came up behind and hooked the dog's collar in his hand, and while Mrs. Burns swept crumbs into a piece of the broken plate, he took the dog outside and tied it up again to the metal chair beside the swimming pool, a blue hole in the front yard filled with birch leaves and brown water.

Buck's dog had returned to Maine that morning by air from Florida, and Mr. Burns had gone to pick it up in the cargo claims. His truck broke down, and he had to take his wife's old Plymouth Fury to fetch the animal in Bangor, a bristle of black wire-hair drugged and fouled in a loaner cage. On the way home, while Mr. Burns dozed with the car running in the parking lot of the Cheese House, the dog woke and chewed out the upholstery in the back seat. When at last Mr. Burns pulled into the Bungalows, the dog ran wheezing down to its old haunts on Second Summer Street and mounted the Greens' Pekingese. The dog also killed a cat, which fortunately belonged to no one.

When he came back indoors, Mrs. Burns, without turning around, asked him for a corkscrew. In his slow no-thinking way, Mr. Burns tried to mount her from behind. She walked away toward the sink, and left him hunched there. "Get off me, Buzz, it's not the time," she said.

"I know it," he told her in his high voice, straightening up.

She made an explosive sound between her teeth, which ended with a crooked smile. "You can't do much, anyway," she said. "Where's that wine?"

"It's behind you," he said.

"Oh, my God, you're going to give them Ripple?"

He looked at the bottle. "It's wine, isn't it?"

"I guess; you could piss in a glass, those girls wouldn't know the difference from Blue Nun." She stubbed out her cigarette in a seashell.

Mr. Burns's face emptied, and his blue eyes closed. This peacefulness came from the Thorazine he took every day, by arrangement with the court officer and Mrs. Burns, who wore a metal plate in her head from where Mr. Burns got her accidentally with his Ruger 10/22 rifle one time.

Becky greeted Mrs. Oates in the office and invited her to sit down in Mr. Burns's tweedy chair on wheels. The mourners stood, or sat in straight chairs Becky had lined up against the paneled walls. Becky went back and forth between the office and the kitchenette, bringing in bowls and plates of food. Most of the time she also carried a year-old baby, not the one by the dead man, but a fisherman's child. The dead man's babies had grown up already into wild-looking boys.

Above the mourners' faces on the walls hung Mr. Burns's gallery of animal mounts. He had taken up taxidermy years ago on Dr. Adenoy's advice. Mrs. Oates looked the stuffed animals over and praised them, which pleased the mourners. Mr. Burns had real feeling, it turned out, for animals killed on the island, and he did a good job of lifting them up from ruined victims of Star Route traffic into examples of their species. A gray owl that had once devastated some chickens hung on the wall beside an eight-point buck with some of its velvet intact and white rings around its black glass eyes. There was a cockatoo Mrs. Burns had taught, when it was alive, to recite the Lord's Prayer. A few of Mr. Burns's early efforts hung there, too, including a squirrel he had cut down so neatly it looked like a vole.

The mourners gathered here because it was the natural setting; Buck Burns had lived at the Bungalows all his life until he moved away. Anyone could see they weren't much, a handful of one-room cabins flung down in a clearing of birch woods. Daylight shone in through the knotty pine boards, and no-see-ums bred in the spongy window frames. Mr. Burns had built the place himself, before he got too drugged to drive a nail, and it still held the town's memory of those years when Buck had his parties and the Burnses didn't care who came or what they did.

Now the guests helped themselves to the beer they brought, except Becky and Melody, who, on account of Becky's nursing her baby, pressed Mrs. Burns for wine. Their boys were eight or nine years old, both curly-haired and dirty blond, like Buck; they wore

Sunday suits that looked as if they came from the church basket. A little girl came in with them, and soon they all disappeared out back.

Mrs. Oates was welcome; several people gave her beer. She was pleased with a drink in her hand to listen to stories of the dead man's life and family. Mr. Burns had fallen into a doze with his back up against the refrigerator—the lulling sound of his breathing carried through the door—and Becky was unraveling that history when Burton Martin, a fisherman and the father of the baby Becky was nursing at her breast, stood up to make a speech. "It's too early, Burton," Becky protested, but Burton insisted that he wanted to speak before everyone got too drunk to listen, and finally out of respect for the dead man, everyone gave him their ears. Mrs. Burns came in, and the silence grew until even Mr. Burns roused himself and leaned in his sleepy way on the frame of the door.

Burton stowed his hands deep in his pockets and told Buck's story as far as he knew it. Buck Burns was larger than life and dangerous beyond the treachery of rules or the law, he said. Temptations other boys fought off by the strength of their character rushed through him like blood in a vein. But his wanting nature and good looks brought out the loyalty people from Black Island felt toward the things that were wilder here—sour berries on the barrens, lobsters crawling in the cold ocean, granite cliffs cracking boats like eggshells and dropping yellow-slickered fishermen into the water.

Those who loved Buck—and they were many—always felt they were going to save him. One time when Buck rolled a Corvair, Burton breathed his own breath into Buck's mouth for eighteen minutes before emergency help arrived—fire engine, police car, the helicopter landing right on the straightaway. But Burton hadn't saved Buck—no one had.

When Buck was eighteen, Burton went on, an advertising agency swooped down on Black Island and saw in him what the town had always seen. The agency snatched him up like a mussel off a rock; they made Buck into the picture of a working man with a beer in his hand: a Clammer, a Sardine Packer, a Fisherman with His Dog. Buck Burns was not any of those things, but he gave them what they wanted. Millions of people saw it and wanted it, Buck's fire and aloofness—he sold more beer than any face the agency ever had. They still had the billboard of him drinking up in Bangor, across the street from Freeze's, and even in town you couldn't look at a magazine in the offices of Dr. Adenoy without seeing Buck and a beer in his hand. He used to be on TV, too, until those commercials got outlawed; Buck was too convincing. Burton asked everyone to remember the one of him fishing in a blizzard, alone on the ocean with his thirst. (Mrs. Oates shook her head up and down. She remembered it well, the angry-looking young man, how the ball in his throat rose and fell with simple pleasure from the bottle; it ran for years.) But it was dangerous, Burton told them, to follow where Buck went. Burton himself had tried taking a few beers and his own dog out on his lobster boat, and the dog went over on a haul chain and drowned.

No matter what Buck did, the town was loyal. The time he drove a borrowed car off the end of the wharf and almost wrecked a sailboat, he ended up in jail, but the city council bailed him out in a vote of civic pride. And who didn't remember those drag races out by the straightaway? Buck sailed fearlessly into the dark, past Kartland and Dennis's restaurant at one hundred miles an hour, and faster than anyone he was gone, swallowed up in his own noise. A few men wept and hooted, remembering what it was like out there, and even Mrs. Oates wiped a tear from her eye with an end of her boiled wool jacket.

Burton hung his head and said that Buck Burns was a treasure and the town had lost him; at least when he died, he took no prisoners, by God. Burton rattled the pockets of his pants and brought up some of his trinkets—a shark's tooth, copper-plated ball bearings—and turned them over in his hand.

Then he asked the mourners to reach out their arms to each other. It seemed like two minutes before anyone could do it; touching was hard. Mrs. Burns left the room. Finally Mrs. Oates reached out her hands to Becky's and Melody's hands and squeezed. Others followed along. Even Buck's boys came in and awkwardly embraced their mothers before helping themselves to the ambrosia.

When the touching was over, Mrs. Burns came back to join the conversation. The subject was her favorite: what a wild man Buck was. She stood in the middle of the office, lit a cigarette, then squinted through smoke at Becky and said, "Ask me what happened to all the money he made."

Mrs. Oates leaned forward on her chair. Becky pulled up her shirt and exposed a surprisingly large, ruddy nipple, which she offered to the baby. Her eyes rolled up.

"He pissed it away, every penny," Mrs. Burns said grandly.

The baby attached itself for an instant to the breast, pulled away, and looked at Mrs. Burns. Then it—another boy—climbed down off Becky's lap and crawled over to the cords that ran to the neon sign out front.

Not everyone believed that Buck had pissed away every penny of the money he made from those beer commercials, a hundred thousand or a million, however much it really was. When checks used to come from the agency, Becky and Melody suggested uses for the money—snowmobiles, dope, groceries, trips up to the Bangor Mall—and Buck had shared it freely while it lasted. Now the future swelled, and if there was any money left, the fate of their two boys or any other children who turned up probably hung on the thread of Mrs. Burns's interest.

Mrs. Oates removed her shoes and crossed her bare feet in Mr. Burns's chair. She pressed the pink end of her tongue against a narrow space between her front teeth. "That's the way with so many in show business," she said, sweeping in Mrs. Burns, Becky, and Melody with a nod. "Following the star is a trail of broken hearts."

Becky and Melody smiled and sipped their wine, but Mrs. Burns's head shot up. "Buck went to Miami by himself," she corrected the guest. "He was going to shoot those commercials in the Keys."

Mrs. Oates nodded. "You don't have to tell me about Miami," she said. "I've lived down in Daytona, near the raceway. You don't know what you've got right here: four seasons and real people." She looked around her, taking them all in.

"Miami's a good town," Burton Martin put in. "I spent a couple of days there when I went to Disney World."

Mrs. Oates lifted an eyebrow in surprise. Burton looked like a man who got up every day of his life at four o'clock in the morning and went alone to the water to haul lobster traps.

"I don't care two cents for Walt Disney World," Mrs. Burns told him. "I've got to settle Buck's estate and collect his cremains. I want to see some things he seen—Naples, Florida, the Keys, the Dry Tortugas. I'm taking his postcards with me."

Nobody challenged her. Nobody knew much about Buck after he went to Florida, except that he must have liked it there. Nothing was ever heard from him again for seven or eight years until word came that he was dead. (The word came to Mrs. Burns from a man named Mr. Pinks, who called and said Buck had died suddenly in the motel he lived in down there; drugs had been hard on his heart. Death coming suddenly at thirty seemed for Buck Burns like a natural cause; everyone was struck, but no one questioned it.)

Silence enlarged around Mrs. Burns like a bubble, swelled and broke as she scratched her lighter with her thumb and lit a cigarette.

"You going to bring the ashes home?" Burton finally asked.

"If he wanted to stick around here forever he would've," Mrs. Burns said, then she added with a sudden spark, "But I might do it, anyway, scatter him out over the straightaway."

A few of the men laughed appreciatively. Melody clicked her tongue, stood up, and walked off into the kitchenette. In a few seconds she was back with a bottle of wine; she poured some out for herself and Becky. Mr. Burns leaned against the door, turning an old bone over in his hands. Mrs. Burns captured his blurred face in her gaze, then looked around the room and said, as if in her own defense, "*He* can't leave the state, he's got his parole."

"It's not parole, I'm on medication!" said Mr. Burns in his high voice.

Mrs. Burns turned on him with the full force of her rage. "You think you're free to go as you please? People have a right to know what you are!" she shouted.

The mourners turned to hear. What was a man after he shot his wife on his own front porch, and had to live with her for twenty-one years afterward, medicated to within an inch of unconsciousness? Mrs. Burns didn't say. Her eyes darted back and forth across the faces arranged along the walls of the office, the animal mounts and underneath them the faces of the mourners. "And anyone who criticizes Buck for getting cremated, that's just how I want it when I go," she said loudly. "That's just how I want it. No religion! No prayers! Just a sack of soot."

"Amen," said Mr. Burns.

"You want me to help you get your stuff together?" Becky asked her.

"I'm not going on vacation," said Mrs. Burns. "All I want is my can of hairspray and a nightgown. I want to take those postcards Buck wrote. That's all." Then she went off alone to gather those things up.

Mrs. Burns, Mrs. Burns! The mourners shook their heads and explained for the benefit of Mrs. Oates that Buck's mother was raised years ago in the clutch of religion. Instead of school she went around the windy outer islands climbing granite hills with a Bible and pamphlets in her mittens; she learned to count by adding souls. Her mother, an old bulb-eyed Canadian, single-handedly ran the Church of the Nazarene and made Mrs. Burns ride out on the mail boat in every weather. Over time most of those fishing families embraced the notion of a wrathful God.

Mrs. Burns came out to save Mr. Burns on Rockrib Island when they were both fifteen. His pa was trawling at sea. She had a certain fire from her upbringing and a highly developed sense of vengeance, it turned out. In the years before he shot her, she almost drove Mr. Burns crazy with her rages, and it all went from her into Buck; her blood was in him and made him who he was.

Mrs. Oates never had to move from Mr. Burns's chair. People milled around her and brought her beer; they told her about Buck, how he had a unit of his own at the Bungalows from the time he was nine or ten years old; that was the best the Burnses could do to protect their son from themselves. Buck raised himself, almost; at seventeen, he already had two sons. The police chief and Dr. Adenoy, both drawn to Mrs. Oates, recalled for her the night the first baby was born to Becky: Buck landed in the hospital, too. He'd gone out for a ride with Melody, which ended when he skidded off the Star Route and ruined her face with shards of glass. Dr. Adenoy numbed her with thirty-six shots of lidocaine and pulled out most of the shards with a needle, but Melody could still show where bits of glass came up in her face from time to time.

Some people believed that if only Buck could have seen that

first baby boy, Becky's, naked and stippled with cold, his tiny arms rising straight up in the incubator, he might have wanted to be a father. But his eyes were covered with bandages, and he was unconscious. Blame spread from Melody to Becky. Those girls were crazy fools! people said. Mixing with Buck Burns! The next winter both girls were steering strollers, riding Buck's babies all around town as if they were jacked-up cars.

Mrs. Oates wondered about Mr. Burns. Becky said things went wrong for him years ago. He used to run the Bungalows when they were a lodge, back when hunters used to come up weekends from Portland or Boston and sit up all night in the office, drink beer and bourbon, and lay log after log on the woodstove. Some didn't know to chase deer that ran gut shot. Mr. Burns could hear deer moo in the woods; he smelled their musk; he could spot a scrape in a birch tree twenty feet away. It was the best thing about him, Becky said, the way he gutted a deer on the spot and put the heart and the liver in a plastic bag in his jacket and cut out the glands and brought even pretty big ones in around his shoulders, still hot on his neck, and butchered them himself. For years he weathered the storms Mrs. Burns kicked up and got the city men in and out in a day and a half with a few steaks from deer he had hung and cured before.

"Venison—yum!" said Mrs. Oates in an encouraging tone.

The accident happened when Buck was around nine, Becky said. Mr. Burns didn't come home all night, and Mrs. Burns came out to the front porch, wiping her hands on a dishtowel, to look for him. He testified in court that he took her for a white-tail deer, and grazed the skull above her eye with one of the lead slugs he used.

Mrs. Oates put a hand to her heart. "Horrible—horrible!"

The jurors understood that a man hunting white-tails with an anticipating mind can see anything he needs to see, antlers in the chokecherry, the white tail in a dishtowel. That's just how the hunter thinks. The verdict was bad luck for Mrs. Burns: she talked too much in court, unraveled too many ancient arguments, and threw the judge and jury into further sympathy with Mr. Burns. But the incident ate away at her. She filed her own civil case and won the right to keep Mr. Burns medicated for life.

Mrs. Oates laughed frankly and shook her head up and down.

On medication Mr. Burns was still recognizable, but more subdued, Becky said. He slept seventeen or eighteen hours a day with his squirrel skins and slabs of wax molded in the shape of wildlife. No one knew how Mr. Burns breathed in there, with the chemicals he used to kill the fleas and lice, the fumes that hung on him of almonds and formaldehyde. He was prohibited from hunting, either by the court or Mrs. Burns, although once in a while at night he went out into the woods and shined some deer, just to get a look at them. Sometimes Buck used to go along.

When the boys were born, first Becky moved into the Bungalows, and then Melody. They took bungalows instead of regular child support and lived like a kind of family, even after Buck left them all and moved to Florida. The Bungalows didn't rent much, anyway. New deer laws came in, and the paying hunters went fishing on the Allagash, or up to Greenville where the blackflies bit like dogs.

Mrs. Oates expressed no interest in moving from her chair, and Becky brought her food on a plate and another beer. Mrs. Oates filled in the blanks of the conversation and speculated on the future of the Burnses. They might separate, Mrs. Burns might stay in Florida, remarry; Mrs. Oates knew from her own experience that the loss of a loved one set you free. Becky and Melody leaned close to hear above the ruckus in the office. Some young men were recounting with the police chief and the doctor certain remarks Buck Burns got off to cops ten years ago, simulating with grinding sounds in their throats the trajectory of doomed cars.

Mrs. Oates let it leak that she had an insurance settlement from Mr. Oates, who died of diverticulitis in Boston. She could go anywhere she wanted; she was looking for a fresh start and a simple life. She wanted four seasons and real people, and she dreamed of opening up a bed and breakfast in a place like this. Melody raised her glass and drank, her eyes narrow, imagining, but Becky jumped at it. Why *not* the Burns Bungalows? Why not here?

Mrs. Burns had never been interested in keeping up the Bungalows, and now that she was leaving, she brought back dark memories: a cold person walking out onto a front porch in the woods holding a dishtowel in her hands during the season when the only white that mattered was the tail end of a deer. Who was the crazy one? Then she kept him drugged for years.

And Mrs. Burns *was* leaving: she came in with a small pink valise in one hand and a cigarette in the other. She found Mr. Burns dozing in the doorway and pulled on one of his earlobes to wake him. He opened his eyes and wiped his face with the back of his hand. "I'm going to see to Buck; you brook it here," she said, and kissed him. It left a red mark on his cheek.

She climbed into her Fury and shot off to the airport. After she left, Burton said it was too bad no one had put Mrs. Burns to bed or sedated her. Now she was gone, he felt they would never see her again.

By the time Mrs. Burns left, it was almost five o'clock. Fred Green poured drinks from Mrs. Oates's bottle into paper cups and passed them around. Mrs. Oates never moved from Mr. Burns's chair. Conversation flowed from her like a liquid. She talked to everyone and ate some of everything Becky brought her on a plate.

The town was sitting, she said, on a gold mine; this pristine beauty was a treasure—the blueberry barrens, the granite cliffs, the lobsters. "It wouldn't take much to turn this place around," she observed, looking around the office in a professional way. "You want to get new blood in. Those Arctic Cats, cross-country skiers." She gestured at the walls, at the gallery of animals. "Even these stuffed animals might be a draw if the rooms were clean."

The mourning went on late. Some rougher stories came up about Buck and some other girls. Mrs. Oates did an impression of Melody, while Melody was in the bathroom: turned her head to one side and pulled a wineglass out of her nose. Even Becky laughed.

Fred Green took down Mr. Burns's stuffed owl from its pin on the wall and laid it on the space heater, where it burst into flame. Fire sprayed out onto the wood floor; a blue line rolled across the boards. Some of the men put it out with bottles of beer. Melody took the stag's head off the wall and leaned it up in a chair behind the front desk. She cocked an imaginary rifle and said, "That you, dear?" Mr. Burns, wherever he was, must have heard the mourners laughing. The walls of the office shook.

In the middle of it all, an animal noise drifted in from the yard. Becky jumped up and ran out of the office screaming. Melody and Burton followed her out, but Mrs. Oates stayed where she was.

The air was already deep blue over the yard, striped black by the birch trees. Buck's dog ran loose, kicking up dust from the ground where Becky's baby lay facing upward a little distance from the swimming pool. The baby was howling and yelling, and Becky ran toward it. It was hard to tell what had happened. The dog crouched near the baby, barking and making noises in its throat, jumping up and running around in a circle, and crouching down again. Becky ran across the uneven yard, veering toward the baby in the pixilated manner of the dog. She reached down to grab her baby, and the dog rushed her, rose up into the air, and bit her on the hand. Becky tore her hand away, and her lips peeled back as if she might bite the dog, but instead she put her hand in her mouth and sucked. Her face looked wild with tears and blood.

Melody moved up behind the dog and hooked her hand under the collar. She pulled it away from Becky and tied it by its leash to the metal chair beside the swimming pool.

The baby yelled, but it didn't look punctured anywhere. Becky held it in her arms, put her breast in its mouth, and sucked on her own hurt hand to draw off the blood. Chief Farnsworth stepped out of the office, hitched up his pants, and cited Becky for neglecting a baby. Burton also spoke roughly to her. What was the goddamned baby doing out in the dark near the swimming pool? The dog was probably saving it. Becky stood and listened, hiccupping as her sobs wore down, her hand in her mouth, the long baby in her arms, its head up inside her shirt, its mouth sucking hard. She looked at Burton in an even way, then she turned and walked back to the office with the baby and shut the door.

"Is she going to be okay with it?" someone asked.

"It's her baby," snapped Melody.

"You ought to go on after her, Burton," Chief Farnsworth said, but Burton said, "Do I look crazy?"

Dr. Adenoy told Melody to go wash Becky's hand off and bandage it; he would come by in the morning.

Burton said he had to get up early, but no one paid attention, and in the end he just walked home, down the hill to town. After Burton left, Melody asked the mourners angrily what kind of man was he, to talk that way to Becky? But everyone already knew what kind of man Burton was. He was the most hardworking and decent young man in town, except in the matter of Becky and the new baby, and even Becky herself didn't hold that against him. Melody went off to get her bottle of peroxide. On the way to her bungalow, she saw their boys—her son and Becky's—in the blue darkness, playing a game called Bear in the Woods. The girl chased the boys, waving a board stuck through with a nail.

Becky opened the door to the office and closed it behind her. Everything looked destroyed. Mr. Burns's taxidermy was strewn around on chairs, the floor was sticky with ambrosia and beer, and the table was covered with bottles, plates, and ashes. In the center of Mr. Burns's chair on wheels, a dark circle spread, where Mrs. Oates had wet it. But the guest herself had gone.

The dog never settled down. It yowled and whined and threatened the mourners, dragging the chair it was tied to screeching across the concrete. A knot of men argued that the dog would never get over Buck's death, a dog never did, and the kindest thing was to shoot it quick. Mr. Burns could stuff it in Buck's memory. Mr. Burns must have sensed the opportunity; it drew him out of Buck's bungalow with an old ranch rifle, and he joined them. With a rapturous gesture, Mr. Burns lifted his rifle to his shoulder for the first time in twenty years. But he turned the gun on the mourners. "Git on!" he shouted. "Go on home!"

That was the end of the party; the mourners left from there. Mr. Burns sat down on the concrete apron around the swimming pool with his rifle in his lap. The dog stood facing him, and barked all night.

Orpheus Crossing

It sounded like eternity—the sun's interminable plucking,
plucking, plucking at the water's strings,

their one continuous chord. It was torment
to witness this devotion to an instrument,

knowing he'd lost his touch, knowing the skills in the bone
plectrum of his neck fell short of the sun's

flash and dazzle. But—no. That was illusion:
the sun didn't perform, and the ocean

only unwound its vast abstract design; like lace
patterned on emptiness and compelled to embrace

it, the surface caught his eye. He wanted
to lower his gaze, but how to escape the constant

needling of sunlight? Night and day it penetrated
every nerve. It left his sight so rent

with glaring holes, he couldn't so much as dream
of the water's dark depths...Beneath

the sun's brilliance, he imagined he looked like
a note, dropped from its composition. But what sight

could accurately read him? No key,
no time signature—no more than a flagging demi-

semiquaver. Now he felt what his songs
must have felt, expelled, breath by breath, from his tongue.

Could a song control its destination? He
opened his mouth and it was filled with the sea.

Latch

Only God can make a tree

"THIS GROVE LACKS AN ALTAR." —So Latch built
A temple and an altar.

Templum aedificavit.
How shall I remember the use of his tools?

(A coffin-maker among the Immortals.
What a scream!)

—Where *is* that Latch now?
Will I see him again in his shadowy cave
On this purgatorial mountain of memory?
And the other immortal hosts: John Skermo,
The gardener; Mary Snorak, the fat cook
In her great sack (500 lbs); and lonesome Jack
The parts-man who loves her and can take a joke?

In the far dark at the back of Latch's shop
Against a rock wall, is the turning-lathe
Which Latch powers by hand, Egyptian fashion.
With a strung bow, Latch makes knops and flowers—
As it is written (*Exodus* 25): "A knop and a flower."
On the living rock above his gigantic
Lathe there shines, bright from sharpening and use,
A graded series of knives. For sure, kid!

Latch is one guy who KNOWS THE USE OF TOOLS!
(A gentile—to be frank.) How shall *I* remember?
Latch says: "IF A TEMPLE IS TO BE ERECTED,
A TEMPLE MUST FIRST BE DESTROYED..."
(All this writing follows from that.)

"Then, do not rebuild it!" says Skermo, the gardener.
"The whole idea of Justice has taken
A wrong turn," he goes on, "no longer sacralizing
Justice *as such,* nor truth, but PAIN. Only God,"
Concludes the gardener, "can make a tree."

"Do not rebuild it!" says Mary Snorak, the cook.
"That there exists a Hell, does not surprise me;
But that Justice made it is beyond belief."
Then Mary Snorak exits sidewise for a smoke
Under a tree and Jack dies laughing again.

"DO NOT REBUILD IT!"—By the waters of
The Mississippi where it flows past Babylon,
Under the burdened willows that are there,
Latch was a mystery. And (as I thought),
"Aphrodite is in his bed." Latch limped.
"Aphrodite must like men who limp," I surmised.
So I learned to limp.

                —What's Latch making now,
Our only coffin-maker on the mountain?
(A year or two ago—not long!—I began to SEE
DISTINCTLY a common world, the meaning of all song,
As when on an island-mountain, high above
The *Wunderkammer* of ocean, the night wind
Shifts offshore in the hour before dawn and
The night air, *dilectissima,* brightens and clears....)
Among shadows, at his lathe, Latch is not sad.
Ingenious cripple with a trophy wife
He is the sole source in the afterlife
Of knops and flowers for the mortuary trade.

Opossum

In the chapel
of the Catholic hospice
we listened to the list
of those who had died
in the past six months.
I waited to hear
the name I had
so missed hearing.
A woman seated in back
comforted a weeping
man, her tears hidden,
"I told you this would make
you feel better. You did
everything you could."

Night came on slowly.
The streetlights flickered
as we made our way home.
Somewhere between purple
and black she spoke
the first words since
we started back.
"Turn on the lights,
it's getting dark."
A few yards ahead,
something was in the road.
It could have been
a shredded tire,
or discarded shirt.

Quickly passing into
the oncoming lane,
I saw it raise

its bloody head,
teeth bared,
eyes shining.
I was not the one,
I had been careful.
But it was dying,
a beaten Job
on a heap of its own
broken bones, looking at me,
screaming blasphemies
to its God. I drove on.

Seduction

You and I lay together on a grassy bed
while one sparrow chased another from a limb.
A bumblebee left a flower he seduced,
and flew away covered in her scent.
I reached my lips to catch your lips before
they turned away. "Just a kiss, please a kiss."

"It always starts the same way, with just a kiss,
then maybe a nibble, soon we're in bed.
I know I should stop now, end it before
it begins." My tongue up your limb,
climbing your thigh, drunk with the scent
of sweet sun-warmed skin, feeling flesh seduced.

My mind began to wander, as you were seduced
though I never told (my mouth filled with a kiss).
I dreamed about the ocean's salt sea scent
and infinite horizon. From the seabed
a scaly creature climbed on newly grown limb.
Feathers formed, turned to hairs, and before

the kiss ended, a man stood where fish stood before.
I'm sorry I didn't tell you. I was seduced
into fantasy, as we groped limb in limb,
about all the human beings who kiss
like we kiss, and have kissed in bed,
on horses, in cars, on grass, in water, scent

of summer rain mixed with the human scent
of sweat sweet excitement I've felt before.
We should have made love, that morning, on that bed.
The air was warm, the light danced on leaves seduced
by gentle winds, I started with the perfect kiss.
You sat, anxious, a bird on a swaying limb.

Were you distracted by wind moving a limb?
All the ingredients for love, with the scent
of danger from a public eye, mixed in a kiss.
I know you have been this close before,
and your mother, her mother, fathers seduced.
For thousands of years humans lay in this bed.

Let me caress you, kiss before kiss.
These lines are our limbs, to be seduced,
these scented words our licks, this page our bed.

Mercury

A vial of it: dusty, warm
From being held so long
In my hand; the little cork that fit

So well, the cap I would undo
In secret, sprawling on the floor
Of the basement, recalling a scene

From Kafka, or glancing in horror
At the old vermilion volume
On Chinese torture, or savoring

The sage-green suede
Of the Rubaiyat, before I ever
Got to Freud. The same dust

Gilded the Harvard Classics,
Uniform in their jackets,
Their leather dry and glossy,

While the glass vial beckoned
With its mysterious fluid
That could bifurcate and scatter,

Rolling, pausing, pooling,
Some dots escaping
Into cracks in the linoleum,

But most of them retrieved,
Succumbing to each other
As I gathered them together

With the slightest pressure,
The liquid growing dimmer
Each time it was restored,

Its ratio of loss too minor,
Too gradual, for Father
To suspect what I had done.

Why was it there, hiding
On his desk behind a pipe
With the face of Mephistopheles?

What experiment forgotten,
Abandoned, untried, what badge
Of glory or failure did it signify,

That small, heavy vial
Whose promise was a murky
Wave of buoyancy, an innocence

Of having, of breaking—
Creating without consequence
Droplets forsaking

The sea whence they came
Without a seam, or cry of protest,
Or any sound of severance

At the source, the minuscule
Remainder a reminder of the refusal
To be destroyed, the singularity

Of every silver bead that briefly
Lived apart from the whole
Before merging and returning

To the vessel I would hold
And shake and spill, and finally
Refill, in a ritual of parting,

Pouring being into
Being, pondering its nature
In the open field of my hand,

My limited supply of a substance
Infinite in its divisibility
And equally indivisible,

An unborn mass of matter
Immortal and mute as the sleeping
Figure eight (not a number,

Really, but the god of numbers)
That Father drew on paper,
Never closed so never ending,

Though once he said to me
In the morning, just as the light
Began to swim through my shade,

Do you think I will always be here?—
As if he were unlocking a door
Between us; and what could I say,

Either way it was unspeakable,
And how could he know
His question altered everything,

That the earth began to change
As the thought of his being no more
Took root, dividing him

From me, from the sky I appealed to,
Unanswered: O god of alchemy
And currency, patron of traders,

Travelers, and thieves, inventor
Of the lyre, master of dreams,
Leader of the Graces, bearer

Of the message that tears
Odysseus from Circe, Aeneas
From Dido, guardian of the departed,

Do not quicken my heart with hope
Anymore, but if you do remember
That I, like the metal you give

Your name to, rejoin if pulled asunder.

Translations from the Irish

for Cathal

Ó Searcaigh, granted one wish by the fairy youth,
wants nothing, so help me, but one dropdead kiss from the youth,
but how can he forget Jack Nolan

who wished away Death for all mankind, Falcarragh's
    own Jack Nolan
whose uncharacteristically generous wish
trapped Death in his fisherman's duffle, a large-hearted wish

though it ended poorly, leaving the old with inexhaustible
    sufferings
and the young to put up with those same everlasting sufferers.
So Jack Nolan reluctantly released Death

from the duffle, returned to the people of Donegal their longed-
    for deaths.
Something smaller, then, thinks Ó Searcaigh, maybe a single day
in which everyone is happy, just one day

in which each of us gets what we've most desired—
why not unite all separated lovers in a Feast Day of Desire?
But even this humbler wish gives pause: might not we get what
    we want

and find we've ruined our lives, never again holding those we want?
The fairy agrees: life can be fucked up good if the wrong prayer's
    satisfied.
Better, says Ó Searcaigh, to wish for one moment when we're all
    satisfied

with what life gives us, one instant when everyone everywhere
    tastes

joy's full measure, sunlight on our backs or the taste
of Tipperary honey, oh anything, anything,

that brings a moment's bliss, anything
that quickens us to gratitude—scent of heather incense on a hike,
or a passing truck that pulls over, letting the hitchhiker

climb to the cab. Ó Searcaigh wishes this. And it comes to pass.
For one girl, it's a twilight of thrushes near a mountain pass;
for a child playing in the muck at Muckish Gap, it's his made-up
     song;

for his mother, picking wildflowers, it's hearing the boy sing;
for one who's pushed words all day across unignitable pages it's
     the words
seized by the mad pulse of a poem; and it's the clear pure word

of spring water from the family well for one home at last. At that
     moment
the fairy flies to Ó Searcaigh, wild with kisses. Oh, shared
     moment
when we all enjoy together this heaven of earthly delights.
     It can't last,

can it? No. No, it can't last longer than heaven ever lasts.

Broughtonia

in memory of F.C. (1965–1991),
who died of AIDS complications

But there under the dark eaves
of rain forest, we found *Broughtonia,*
its crimson petals aflame,
its yellow throat, veins hinting purple,

rising to a sanguine corolla surrounded
by sepals as crinkled as mourning crepe.
We followed a path lengthened slash by slash,
the islanders swinging *machetes* in front of us.

We were told how Broughton's hands trembled
when he sighted those orchids languishing;
as he sketched, his nervous pencil
exaggerated the crumpled edge of every bloom.

We, too, had learned to exaggerate.
That night in Montego Bay,
we told the others we had seen dozens;
in New York, we said hundreds.

Today, we might have imagined the wind
licking us back into the Gully,
our hands as uninhibited as those petals.
No. I can no longer imagine. I choose not to.

Thinking of Gorki While Clearing a Trail

It wasn't exactly raining but
a little wetness still dribbled down.
I had been reading and sorrowing
and set out with the dogs as an antidote.
They went ahead snuffling in the leaf plaster.
Despite the steady snick of my clippers
boletus mushrooms kept popping soundlessly
out of the ground. How else account for
the ones with mouse bites out of the caps
when I doubled back on my tracks?

The animals have different enzymes
from us. They can eat amanitas
we die of. The woodpeckers' fledglings
clack like a rattle of drumsticks each time
crumpled dragonflies arrive and are thrust
into the bud vases of their gullets.
The chipmunk crosses in front of me
tail held up like a banner. Who knows
what he has in his cheeks? Beechnuts
would be good, or a morsel of amanita.

Gorki disliked his face with its high
Mongol cheekbones. *It would be good to be
a bandit,* he said, *to rob rich misers
and give their money to the poor.* Saturnine
Gorki, at the 1929 International Congress
of Atheists. By then, he was famous but
twice, in his teens, he tried to kill
himself. Called before an ecclesiastical
tribunal and excommunicated, he declared
God is the name of my desire.

The animals have no Holy Synod to
answer to. They simply pursue their vocations.
In general, I desire to see God lifting
the needy up out of their dung heap
as it is written. I did not seek this
ancient porcupine curled in the hollow
of a dead ash tree, delicately encoded
on top of a mountain of his own dung,
pale buff-colored pellets that must have
taken several seasons to accumulate.

At this moment, I desire the dogs, oblivious
so far, not to catch sight or scent of him.
I am the rightful master of my soul
Gorki said, and is this not true of the porcupine?
Born Aleksei Maksimovich Peshkov
he chose his own name—*gorki*—bitter
and a century later I carry him
like a pocket guide on this secret trail
clearing and woolgathering as we go.

GEORGE GARRETT

False Confessions

The author of this story had other plans for me. In his, alas, typical ignorance and ineptitude, he decided to use me (one more time!) as the heavy, a really bad guy in a bleak and downbeat story that most likely would gross you out or, in any case, would sure enough give you the willies, as they say, troubled about the essential nature of humankind as represented, exemplified by me, an antihero if there ever was one.

You probably don't know me from Adam or Adam's rottweiler. And I can't blame you for that. How would you know me, and why would you? I ask you! I don't intend to bother you, to cover the whole thing. All you really need to know at this point is that I am precisely what I seem to be (how many of you can make that claim?)—a fictional character, another imaginary person who usually ends up doing and being whatever some author, real or so-called, wants the aforesaid character (usually no more substantial or dimensional than a shadow) wants him or her to be.

There are, of course, many disadvantages to life (and death) as a fictional character. I could go on and on about the subject and soon generate overwhelming ennui all around. But you can easily imagine most of the pains and problems and disappointments. Not least of which is the almost complete absence of free will. Whether I am willing to admit it or not, most of the time I have to be what my author wants. More to the point I have to be and to do what he wants even when it challenges common credibility and violates the sacred and sanctified rules and guiding principles of literary criticism. Which means (think about it; go figure) I not only can't save myself, but also I can't come to his aid, either. I end up having to take the blame, together with my author, for whatever he makes me do or leave undone. That is really and truly unfair. And note the irony of it: I am composed, in fact and in any fiction I find myself involved in, of the figments and fragments of his conscious and unconscious obsessions. He may well think that he is freer than I am. If so, that is purely and simply a delusion.

It would be funny if it weren't so damn personal.

I said chances are you have never heard of me. Fine, I never heard of you, either. (In a culture firmly based on celebrity, that puts us both at a distinct disadvantage.) I never claimed to be a Captain Ahab or a Huck Finn, not Bech or Rabbit Angstrom or Zuckerman, either. My name is John Towne, and I have "starred" as the (pardon the expression) protagonist in maybe half a dozen short stories as well as in the widely reviewed and yet little-known novel *Poison Pen*. Most of the people who reviewed that book found something or other nice to say about the author, but they seldom, if ever, spoke or speak well or kindly and gently of me. *The New York Times Book Review* called me "a low-life crank"; "a lecherous, misanthropic failed academic," opined *The Chicago Tribune*; someone writing for *The Village Voice* called me "an exceptionally sleazy picaro." And on and on in that vein. Probably the strongest and meanest judgment (it would be slander if I were real) appeared in *The Greensboro News* in a review by Fred Chappell, who identified me as "a loathsome, racist, sexist, crude, and gruesome creep."

Meanwhile the author who invented me was being described in other terms. Here is how *The New York Times Book Review* elected to characterize him: "He is a well-respected writer with a prestigious academic position—he's Henry Hoyns Professor of Creative Writing at the University of Virginia."

Bully for him! Pushing seventy, he makes about as much as a junior corporate executive fresh out of college.

Do you know what he originally had in mind for me in this story? He planned to put me back into an academic setting and context (where I have done hard time before—"an academic gypsy and con man," *The Roanoke Times* named me) so that I could be poorer than he is. He planned to involve me and expose me in a singularly repellant story. It tells how I set out to seduce and betray the wife of a friend and colleague of mine, a poor old guy who is suffering from Alzheimer's. My motivation, such as it was (my author not planning to go too deep into the subtleties of motivation), at least at the outset, revenge. I want to hurt him because I did not get the promotion (and tenure) that I talked myself into believing that I richly deserved, even though I had not done anything to earn it and even though he, alone, among the entire senior faculty, had always been generous and friendly to me and was probably the only member of the whole frigging department who thought I had any redeeming social value and who would have spoken up for me if he hadn't already been diagnosed with Alzheimer's.

In the story, according to the author, he, this suffering and slowly dying professor, was the scapegoat I invented. None of the others was particularly vulnerable, and, anyway, they wouldn't let me close enough to do them any harm.

Another motivation the author laid on me was that the wife in question was really good-looking. Extraordinary. Exceptionally attractive. I was to observe and/or remark, somewhere in the story, that except for her golden hair she was a first-rate knockoff of Cindy Crawford. (That would serve to characterize me as a guy who took popular culture a little too seriously, at face value. Which, in fact, is true.) This second motivation, lust, would tend to add to the ambiguity of my situation: that I was using the payback motive to disguise the simpler truth from myself and to justify my strong urge to try to seduce his wife while he was altogether defenseless and she was more or less vulnerable.

Another reason that the author planned to motivate me by sexual desire was that he had used this same thing, in other stories and in *Poison Pen,* to explain away my actions. Problem is, this kind of evidence is inadmissible and irrelevant. What I may have done or left undone in the context of another story has no bearing on this one.

What was supposed to happen here was that I would gently insinuate myself into her good graces by helping them in any and all ways that I possibly could—running errands for her, taking care of minor tasks and chores, and baby-sitting the old fart for a few hours while she went off, like a good creative faculty wife, to paint pictures or write poems or throw pots or whatever.

In the story the seduction turns out to be a whole lot easier than it probably would be—for you or for me or for anyone else—in real life. Pretty soon I am regularly having fun and games with her anywhere and anytime I can. Sometimes even right there in the house, in their bedroom. I mean, he has reached the point where he can't remember from one minute to the next; so what do we care if he should walk in on us? And it is all great and wonderful, and I find myself enjoying every minute of it. The author adds some complexity to my motivation by asserting that, in part, I am also getting even with all the beautiful women who have turned me down and/or spurned my amorous advances in a lifetime spent trying to score. Well, he is way off base there. By and large I have never had any problem making out with women, plain or fancy. I like women a lot, and most of the time I know how to get along with them. And that important and undeniable fact does not come across in the story. Let the author say whatever he pleases. My overall record speaks for itself.

What happens to me in the story, as the author sees it, is that I will inevitably fall in love with the woman. I don't mean to, of course (whoever does?), but I can't help myself, and I do so, anyway. And then because I have begun to care for her, I also begin to feel profoundly guilty. Meanwhile, though I am not aware of it yet, she also is tormented with guilt. So there you are with the three of us—the two guilt-ridden lovers and the old guy who has passed beyond all that kind of pain and trouble.

Now, then. You know, and I know, and I suspect even my author does, that most of the time guilt leads nowhere else but to a lot of deeper trouble. When we are feeling really guilty, we quickly discover that we are unable to forgive ourselves. So our first thought is always to unload that guilt onto somebody else, anybody who happens to be handy. As far as I can tell, guilt (not shame, mind you, or sorrow) does nobody any good. Except maybe psychiatrists.

In this particular story that we are talking about, there is a big scene, après some very good and memorable afternoon sex, during which we each try to assuage our guilt with false confessions. I intend to tell the truth, but only a part of it. I don't tell her that I have come to love her. I tell her that the whole thing was just about getting even with her husband and that now that I have done just that, I feel wonderful.

Fighting back with fury, she says the whole thing is truly funny. Because, you see, she never really loved her husband or cared about him one way or another while he was still well and wideawake. She wanted comfort and security, and she got just that. But when he became ill, she cared for him out of guilt. All the time she was ready, willing, and able to be seduced by anybody, the first man who came along. Which happened to be me, but might as well have been the postman.

It's a joke on both of us, she would say, ha-ha. I was not to be allowed to take any pride or pleasure in my seduction of her. And all of my guilt, real or imaginary, was utterly without meaning or implication.

On the way out of the house (why am I described as tiptoeing, for Christ's sake?) I decide to steal something valuable from him. My first thought is his real nice, expensive wristwatch. I could take it right off his arm if I wanted to, and he would never know the difference. But then, instead, the souvenir I take is his Mont Blanc fountain pen, resting on his dusty desk. I mean, why not? He won't be writing anything with it, anyway.

Then the way the story ends is that, even before the academic year is over and done with, the old guy dies. His young wife (did I fail to mention that fact—young? Sorry) puts him in the ground at the old college cemetery. The only plots left available are down at the far end close-by the railroad tracks. Well, at least he can listen to the whistle and rattle of freight trains coming and going. Eternity could be a lot worse.

After the funeral she packs up and takes off. I like to think she has gone to Southern California or Florida or maybe the Gulf Coast. Maybe Mexico. Someplace warm, anyway, where she can stretch out on a beach blanket and show off her incredible figure and pick up or ignore any old geezer she wants to.

I like to think that she sometimes thinks of me.

I am portrayed as thinking these things because I am busy packing up my own stuff to move on to the only job I have been able to get—at a college in miserable upstate New York, Joyce Carol Oates territory, Frederick Busch turf. I will freeze my ass off up there where it stays dark more than half the time.

The reader will think that this serves me right.

In the last couple of lines the reader will also think that this story, in the form of a confession, is presumed to have been written with my newly acquired Mont Blanc pen. Here, at the tag end, I am shown wondering whether or not I will ever write her a letter and what I will find to say in it, assuming I can find out where she has gone.

Even though the author insists he is going through a "dark"

period and can't help himself, I find this story to be too down-beat. I would much rather not be caught up in something so ugly and offensive and heavy-handed. Of course, it is only a slight variation on the familiar and conventional plot in which some-body sets out—on a bet or an impulse, out of anger or frustration or boredom—to seduce somebody else and, either in success or failure, falls in love. The odd little moral of such tales, usually, is the commonplace truth that sometimes there are good conse-quences of bad actions. Well, that's not news. All of us know that much.

Admittedly we have only had time to deal with the general story line here. As my author would be the first to point out, we have neglected to consider the texture and the details, the little things he likes to do that, ideally, add up. Like, for example, plot-ting the pen very early in the story in a brisk, almost casual description of the professor's desk and study. I would notice and admire the pen, among other valuable things, that's all. But it would seem like an old friend when I suddenly decide to steal it. And I have to admit he does a nice little thing with her beautiful blond hair, touched and glowing in the late afternoon sun, on the blue pillowcase just before he (I) offers up his confession.

Now I wouldn't say that my author is completely without any talent. Imagine how that would be for the poor, helpless (pardon) protagonist, prisoner of a complete, no-talent, bumbling fool! There are plenty of those out there. And so it is that even if we are not dealing with an Updike or a Roth or any such, I can never-theless count my blessings. It can always be a whole lot worse, be-lieve me.

One of the great flaws of the story, as the author wrote it, disre-garding my advice, is that he doesn't spend much time or detail on the professor. The story would have more meaning and impact if we had some special sympathy for the old guy. There was a brief scene, later cut during revision, in which we see the professor, with my help and the help of his wife, get dressed to go and teach a class. Which, of course, he can't do, anyway. But there is this little game of getting him ready to go forth into the world and to do something. Only by the time he's ready to go, he has forgotten what it is he was planning to do. The author almost stumbled onto something worthwhile when he decided that the old guy had wonderful clothes and that he looked good in them. We get him dressed; he admires himself in the mirror; and then he wanders around the house, upstairs and down, basement and attic, without rhyme or reason, vaguely wondering what is happening to him. But the author chickened out of that scene.

I could be disloyal and tell you a thing or two about the author, things he would just as soon you didn't know, now and forever. But what good would that do me? Seriously, that is the first and foremost question that you have to ask of anybody, especially including fictional characters. What is in it for him/her? From the school of experience I can tell you that people, human beings, don't do anything either good or evil, without there being something—pride, pleasure, vanity, self-esteem—in it for themselves. Even the purest forms of altruism and sacrifice are tainted. (Know what I mean?) Love, I guess, true love is the coincidental state, the odd and unexpected occasion when the lives and the circuitry of the desires of two people (briefly, briefly) come together and share the same frequency or wavelength. Or else, like happiness, love can be defined as the state of being well-deceived.

What I really hate, though, is being made the public scapegoat for the author's guilt. He heaps troubles on my head in hopes of hiding the grubby truth about himself. You can bet your sweet ass he has done plenty of things (thought, word, and deed) that he ought to be sorry for.

In the various and sundry fictions I have lived in and through, I have been allowed to be happy a few times. And I was even happy at times in this otherwise unhappy story up until, but including, that afternoon. Her beautiful blond hair splashed on the blue pillow. Dust motes dancing in sunlight, the sweet smell and the smooth touch of her. Taste of her still on the tip of my tongue. Even the sound of her voice as she came to curse my name. And myself, ageless and weightless, floating in time as if in flowing water, for once fully satisfied and, for that moment, feeling free. Free at last to tell the truth, to confess all and maybe be forgiven. Which turned out to be exactly what the author had planned for me all along.

GREG GLAZNER

Orchard Bees

Wrung-out, aching, caked with a sweat
he wouldn't claim, living the wrong life,
he shook the branch until the last apple fell,
never glancing at the others, whose backs,
as they gathered, were as arched and gravity-clutched
as his, their gestures in the limbs as solemn,
as exhausted of flight. Bees drifted where he labored:
he imagined taking in that hovering intelligence
humming the way back, the sweetness
welling up inside on its own, that furious
attendant stinging.
               And he dreamed it
resting in his room at dusk, letting bees
drift through the open window like a gold smoke,
lighting on the potted irises, shuttling
weightlessly back out, a tune he'd heard
in his mother's humming before she died,
charming the locusts and the mayflies
of his childhood, and after, from the balcony,
when the girl in flowers sang "Sweet Honey
in the Rock," over a bronze platter of candles.
Even her teeth and tongue were washed with gold.

He craved so much more than the dumb labor
and the daily wish of bees arriving and leaving.
So he roused himself and went back, among the ripening,
to the hive in the dead oak's hollow, and reached
inside the chaos of buzzing, a down all over
his arm like thorns grown fiercely inward.
Then he held a gold fistful of cells, dripping,
the queen rich there in his grip, and felt
the swelling, his hand already alien, a mitt,
he thought, for what was beyond pain, and sweeter.

Swallowing his cries, he stumbled home, the swarm
trailing him like a gold whirlwind on its side,
its force pouring in and out of his palm,
nothing of his sleeve visible, instead a furious,
winged skin made entirely of teeming.

Inside, he felt the writhing of a new life pacing
everywhere, needling him all over, so shivering,
he plucked the wings and legs from the queen, asking
Will you forgive me, little master? and eased her,
alive, back onto the cluster of cells and honey,
and laid it all, not much bigger than a gold wafer,
on his tongue, squinting back his tears. He thought,
Not my will but yours, not my life
but the one that opens everything
in spring, in a singing no one owns.

What filled him then, for hours, an intelligence
shattering itself over his skin, in his mouth,
its voice of little terrified violins awakened
inside him, the sugars dripping from it,
was what he'd always dreamed of being, other,
a home of voices not his own, their harm
and sweetness, sustenance, all the way
at his core, though the swelling in his throat,
though his eyes full of their own closure
would not stay open, his ears turning
to nothing in the hum—particulars failing
the stuffed chair under him his weight
the sense of his mother's round pale face
when he tried to call it back—the stabbing

of his boundaries turning to something else some
black painlessness regret exploding in his place
taking back the whiteness from the walls the hum
he'd allowed inside too much to give but the sense
of his mouth was passing notes a far-off murmur
of blankness eroding even the erasure's feel
and the changing began

           to slow but it wasn't done.
When he was cold, the hive still growing, the throat,
the stopped lungs filled with something like breathing
that wasn't breath, a flurry and a cache
of sweets, a motion living on without him now.
And the amber music, winged, fully bodied, as real
as steamed breath had been in the spring dawn,
streamed in and out the window, a tune nothing
was humming from no one's mouth of bees, winding
out to lay its wash of weightlessness and pain
where it was required, down over the worked land,
and the trees' brief blossoming, over the earthbound,
upward-facing keepers of the trees.

CAROL FROST

Sin

The tree bore the efflorescence of October apples
like the bush that burned with fire and was not consumed.

The wind blew in cold sweet gusts,
and the burning taste of fresh snow came with the gradual dark

down through the goldenrod. The blue and scarlet sky
was gently losing its color,

as if from use.
The towers and telephone poles rose in the distance.

And a decline
of spirit, hearing, all senses; where the mind no longer rests,

dwells, intrigue; and Satan's quick perspective of what lies ahead,
was foretold by the springing back of a bough.

—We'll never know the all of it: nature's manifesto,
the sleight-of-hand in God's light, the invisible,

visible, sinned against, absolved, no matter the enormity
of trying, and Eve's help.

But come just before sunrise and see and taste again
the apple tree coming into fire

—shadow-glyphs on the crystallized grasses,
geese surging above the loblolly pine, the smell of sap—

as if willingly through its long life
it held on to one unclarified passion and grew and regretted
    nothing.

Red Oak Farm

off-season home of a circus elephant

Here, the past forgets
its boundaries, shines
through abandoned objects:
the caved tin roof
of the slave quarters,
wind-beaten planks
and rusted knives
scattered in dust and sand.
Soon, the elephant
will make her slow way
down this path, graze
among the ruins and pines;
each step an indelible print
in the Carolina soil,
where future scientists
may kneel, one day,
and wonder. All live things
leave their trace
in the tangible world:
the cotton mill speaks
a legacy of sweat
and tears; in the air, still,
the muted whine
of carriage wheels and
hoof-beats, infant cries,
the eternal songs
of the enslaved. They are all
here, watching,
as the elephant tears limbs
from the trees, wraps
her ancient trunk
around the crumbling

wooden doorframes.
All around, dark faces
turn skyward to see
her massive form, emblem
of their homeland, in silhouette
against the hazy, southern sun.

TIMOTHY DONNELLY

Scarecrow in Magnolia

We raked until raking puffed our mitts with hot blisters.
Then we desisted. Wind de-raked our raking then,
spilled the tops of our piles, blew new-fallen bronzes

across brief spans of lawn. We worked like the damned:
I the Sisyphus of fall, you the Sisyphus of autumn.
Rakes dropped, we drifted through discarded wrappers

to a graveyard but yards from our unfinished raking, caught
neighbors peering down through parts in high curtains
to catch us there, looking. Oldest stone. Newest stone. Smallest.

One the size of a toaster read: *I bud on earth, to bloom
in heaven.* We drifted back then. With what leaves we could
muster we filled dungarees, a workshirt bequeathed

on a hook in the cellar. For the head: a plastic pumpkin.
And to keep this arrangement from the wind's
undoing, we cut utility twine in five measured lengths,

four for closing the cuffs, one to pass through the belt loops and bow.
We tangled these limbs in the limbs of magnolia.
The head balanced. Night fell. In the scant moonlight

and the light of seven streetlamps, the sealed magnolia buds
seemed a light silver, the peeling bark a lighter silver,
and the lesser branches brittle black. The figure shaking

in the limbs had shed its color, or it was also black.
The stuffed interior. The rumpled thing. The black flower
that we had meant to blossom was, blossoming.

Myself as a Wasting Phoenix

With each rebirth, a little more
is lost. As pounds of feathers turn
to flame—then ash—an ounce, at least,
is bound to blow off.

Take the breast. It may appear
less lushly plumed than myth has led you
to expect. In this unfortunate event,
permit us to apologize

on our bird's behalf. Please excuse
as well: a slackened beak, two dull
and dwindling wings, a blank expression.
We've tried everything,

with no success. Nothing not tried,
we've merely watched it growing
sparse. And worse, we now believe
the bird's internal organs

are equally at risk. Medicine shows
no effect. Transplant impossible,
of course. One cares to keep a distance
between their person

and its cage; we find, this season,
that our exhibit goes ablaze—both
in frequency and force—increasingly.
Sad creature of habit!

Clearly this poor wasting phoenix,
no more intelligent than the wood
grouse or pheasant, has yet to recognize
the cause of its decay,

although some theorists claim the opposite
is true. To their hypotheses
our office has responded disapprovingly.
Everyone's entitled—

even you—but these impartial charts predict
the final flicker of our bird
should occur at noon, the Thursday after next.
A most regrettable loss,

it will require for all concerned
an indeterminate length of time
in which to adjust. Tickets available
for those of interest.

MICHAEL TYRELL

For the World

Whatever it once meant,
no one remembers today.
Trains run according to schedule.
School is in session.
No prophets,
no candle-bearing crowds.

The paper doesn't mention.
The public memory's clean.
The season's all
that remains: October,
a liminal time
before the souls rise.

Once this date was inked
on calendars; it guaranteed
a parade. Even the senators
bowed their heads
when they spoke its name.
Poems trailed its borders like seeds.

Where are the poems,
are they buried too?
This must mean something,
been felt somewhere else on earth,
the early cold, the shortening
hours when the awful, the beautiful, wait to be born.

Perhaps it was private,
still *is* private, forgotten again
once the man with the swaddled box
is gone, has finished crossing the street.
In his arms, the gift is heavy.
Is it not for the world?

JOHN MCMANUS

Stop Breaking Down

At Tin Mill Canal the left headlight burned out. Darker now: eight eyes blinking at the nailing darkness. The sewage treatment plant and its sooty gray sewage-treated smoke rising openly into pinkblack air went grayer. Near the end now nothing to worry about—did you do that, Rootie?—you saboteur you sly bastard you it'll take more than that. We approached the bridge looming tall before us and soaring. Upon the western skyline Venus and a crescent perched above the towers. Line of sight. The radius clutching nightgloom all the darktime; close to the end now, and Tobey tossed his empty beer bottle into the back seat thrusting it against Phoebe's forehead. Clunk. She punched him in the shoulder, and the action of his reflex swerved the wheel in a sharp skid to the right. Watch it, he said. I'm the driver. You're the passenger.

We approached the bridge. Don't see you in the rearview you slow shits. Win. The engine sputtered. Always. He reached beneath his seat for another beer and opened it against the dashboard. Drunk and darting across space. Eight eyes roaming across the gray industrial postdusk dark. Displacement. A moment, I think.

Tobey laughed. Full circle, he was thinking. Isn't that what they call it.

Last call at Sudsucker's was at two. The seven of us had sat in the back by the Atari, two in chairs and five squeezed together on the couch, which we had occupied since dinnertime. The tab was over a hundred dollars. Vince poured out the contents of the final pitcher.

These your songs on the jukebox, man?
Yeah.
Vince and Tobey were playing Maze Craze. My eyes ached from the flashing colors. The bright monochromatic screens. Red and blue dots racing along corridors to the right-hand side of the screen.

Won again, Tobey said.

Get your kicks now, man.

That's nineteen for me.

Just wait till we're on the road.

Phoebe rolled her eyes.

Can't wait, Tobey said.

You're not serious about this race, Adam said. The bartender came to wipe off the coffee table, and they all lifted up their drinks. Adam watched the next maze appear on the screen. He didn't want them to see that he was worried. Around the Beltway. What are they talking about. They're all drunk. How the hell did this get started, he was wondering. You're not serious, he said to them.

Is that a question or a statement of your opinion? Tobey asked.

Adam glared at him.

I'm looking at the video game but I can feel you glaring at me. Answer the fucking question.

You answer my question.

So it was a question.

Jesus help me.

No.

No you're not serious? he asked. The others had stopped their conversation to listen.

No, no you're wrong that I'm not serious. We're serious. You'll be in the car so you'll be serious too. We're all serious. We'll all be serious. We'll all be serious together.

I'm not riding with you, then, he said. Fuck it.

The buses don't run this late, Adam. You can't afford a cab all the way back to Hamilton. You can't even afford the beer you just drank. Can you.

I don't think you should do this.

Whatever.

Shut up, Adam, Ben said. Everyone nodded in agreement.

In the cold air on Fort Avenue we stood by the cars and smoked. Here are the rules, Vince said. We go down Ritchie Highway to exit three and the race starts there. The on-ramp. That's where it starts.

So it ends at the exit three off-ramp, Ben said.

No, Vince said. It ends at the end of the Key Bridge. Go around the inner loop and whoever crosses the end of the bridge first wins.

The people in that car pay the others back for tonight's tab, Tobey said.

That's not fair, Vince said. There's four in your car.

I guess that will be added incentive for you to win.

I should just hitch a ride home, Adam was saying to Phoebe, shaking his head in disgust.

Then do it, she said.

Whose side are you on here?

I'm not on anyone's side, she said, gently nudging his shoulder. I just think it will be fun. You shouldn't be so uptight.

How fast does that baby go? Tobey asked.

Hundred twenty and it don't even rattle. Hundred forty you might start to feel a little shake.

Phoebe rolled her eyes.

Shit, Tobey said.

Shit's ass.

Quit your braggin' and let's see it.

How many miles is it to go around? Ben asked.

I don't know; the numbers don't correspond with the exit signs.

It's gotta be fifty at the least.

At the very least.

We'll do it in half an hour tops, Tobey said.

I'm with Vince, then, Ben said. I wanna do it in twenty minutes.

Tobey drove a turbocharged Cougar. Eighty-nine model year but a ninety-four engine. Black body and a red hood. Surprised they let you across the state line with that ugly hunk of metal, Vince had said when Tobey first moved to Baltimore. Surprised they don't levy a special redneck tax on your ass. He followed Vince's Camaro down Ritchie Highway. No traffic. Vince was running the red lights, and Tobey had to run them too to keep up. He glanced around for cops.

Past the fast-food restaurants and gas stations. Mile-wide strips of pavement. Down the hill to the exit onto the Beltway. Neon idiot lights.

Sprawl.

At the on-ramp Vince screeched his tires as he turned right and accelerated quickly down the ramp. Tobey stayed on his bumper. As they pulled out into the lane we could see Rootie in the back seat of Vince's car flipping us off. He signaled something to us, pointing toward the hood and bumper of Tobey's car. What's the bastard trying to say, Tobey said.

Hell if I know.

Vince sped up to a hundred and went into the left lane. Tobey followed. Vince sped up and slowed down, slamming on his brakes and speeding up and switching to the middle lane and darting around cars. He turned his left turn signal on. He turned his right turn signal on. He turned his rear wipers on.

What a dumbass.

We're gonna win.

When we passed the Harbor Tunnel Thruway the road had more traffic. Tractor-trailers. Vince pulled into the Washington Boulevard exit lane to pass a pickup truck and managed to steer back onto the road barely in time. Adam gasped when the Camaro jolted back into the main lane.

Pass them, I said.

No don't, Adam said.

Just let him drive, Phoebe said. Even more traffic came onto the road after we crossed under I-95. Tobey gripped the wheel. Pass all these fuckers. Steadily smoothly. What they must be thinking. Twice as fast as them at least. Turn their heads. Excitement in their lives. Scared. If they're scared then they'll get out of the way. We felt the car pulling to the left, toward the concrete barrier. Out the side window no look out the front window. Reflection in the night.

Control. Feel it in the air. Stay out of our way.

Phoebe packed the sherlock as we passed Arbutus. Tobey was still following behind the Camaro. Pass them, I said but he was waiting for something to happen. They'll get stuck behind someone, he was thinking. They'll have to brake. Gotta do it when they can't respond.

You got a light? Tobey asked when it got to him.

Use the cigarette lighter, Phoebe said.

You can't light a sherlock with the fucking cigarette lighter, he said.

The Beltway wall had been completed. Infinite sienna squares. Meant to look like something. Adobe maybe. As I lit the pipe the passing wall squares began to dominate all the peripheries. Count them one two six ten no it's far too fast. They're getting away, Phoebe said.

They're not getting away.

Just let him drive, Adam said sarcastically. She glared at him. Just let him drive, he said again.

We bounced along the broken pavement. Sure do see a lot of Maryland license plates in this damn state, Tobey said. The bowl was cashed, and I put it in the glove box. We bounced along the ridging pavement and the CD player skipped on the bumps. Tobey and I clicked bottles together in a toast, beer sloshing out upon our hands and arms. Rebel yell. We passed Frederick Road. We passed Edmondson Avenue. We passed Baltimore National Pike. Phoebe was wrestling with Adam in the back seat, trying to cheer him up, and she snapped his seat belt undone and pinned his arms and neck in a twisted half nelson. He didn't fight back. She pushed him playfully back into his seat, and he refastened his seat belt. We passed I-70. We passed Security Boulevard. Through the cracked window the cool fall air sucked against the glass with a shrill sinister hiss, and every passing car whined lowly in fading Doppler hyperbolas of stunted sound.

Whose idea was this, Adam said. It was Vince's, wasn't it?

Phoebe rolled her eyes.

I don't remember, Tobey said. The dashboard's loose brown plastic rattled loudly.

It was Vince's, Adam said, wasn't it?

Vince wouldn't have been smart enough to think of it, Phoebe said. She rolled her eyes. What the hell is he doing, anyway? she said. The Camaro was in the far left lane, halfway into the left shoulder, the yellow line centered beneath them. Dumbass is gonna get a flat tire.

Blowout at this speed God could you imagine?

The Camaro moved back onto the road. Tobey stayed in the middle lane. There's a car up there in the shoulder, he said.

Cop.

No.

Could be.

No man. This is it.

Huh?

They'll think it's a cop. This is it. Soon now. He counted: Three. Two. One.

The rear of the Camaro swerved twenty degrees to the right as Vince slammed his brakes. Screech. Eighty sixty fifty. We watched them try to right themselves from the side window and then the back windshield as Tobey downshifted to fourth gear and floored the gas. Redline. To the floor. At eighty-five hundred rpms he shifted back up into fifth gear. He shot past the motionless blobs of metal, one hand on the wheel and one hand on the stick, head pressed back against the seat and eyes staring straight ahead as if he were playing an arcade game.

Damn.

We gained more ground.

Damn is that them way back there?

Don't slow down, man.

Adam shut his eyes and made the sign of the cross.

What the hell are you doing? Phoebe said. You're not religious. He didn't answer.

Damn.

Good job.

The car on the shoulder was a rusting engineless truck. A dead black hulk. You lost it for a shadow. This is fast. In the Cougar we sped north along the bulging eight-lane ribbon. If we get pulled over I'm fucked, Tobey was thinking. The red in his eyes. The worried red. Don't know what Adam's worried about. I'm the one going down. Is this Thursday? Chugachugachuga rumble hurdling above the speakers.

Scratchy stringy voices on air: Take me down little Susie take me down. I know you think you're the queen of the underground. He maintained his speed.

Eyes shut no eyes open. We were all getting tired. Tobey was feeling the disturbances in his stomach and the insidious night exhaustion. As he belched sore-throated and loudly the air and inner lining of his stomach churned heavily and slow, the enzymes coating wet pink flesh walls with thick gray mercury—we heard this—fastening themselves to the gas and slime like murky algal muscles. You'll have to take the wheel if I puke, he said.

You better not.

Tobey didn't answer.

I can't see them at all now, Phoebe said. The road was emptier. We passed the Northwest Expressway. We passed Reisterstown Road.

You know, Phoebe said, you never notice the curves. It's a circle but you never see it curving.

But you feel it curving.

We passed Park Heights Avenue. We passed wooded subdivisions and houses sticking up above the wall. Swooosh around the curves. See there are curves. He belched again. We passed Greenspring Avenue. We passed JFX. Above the hum of the engine rose the sounds of old metal rattling and metal against metal in grating metallic friction. Above the hum of the engine rose the whirs and the hammering thuds and thunds of thunder, the whines of rubbed-raw body fronds. The rhythm. Stronger now. Later. Heated motion, and the dull cracked shoulder, the yellow reflections reflecting back in yellow. The wall standing dark hushed hale as rubber tracks pithed the thin magnetic chords of open road.

Why don't you drop me off on York, Adam said. I'll walk to Walter's apartment.

If you wanna just jump out of the car then do it but I'm not stopping.

Come on, Tobey, he said. They're nowhere in sight.

But they will be if I stop to let you off.

Come on, Tobey.

No one spoke as we drove past 83 North, Charles Street, York Road, Dulaney Valley Road. Providence Road. Tobey maintained his speed. He was wondering if something had happened to Vince's car. He was drumming his tongue against his teeth. He was listening to the pains in his lower left quadrant wondering if his spleen was swollen from drinking again before he had fully recovered from mono. He was wondering whether or not he'd get pulled over for reckless driving. Over a hundred and you can spend the night in jail. He could feel the tension in his shoulders forcing his shoulder blades up and outward. He could feel his neck. He could feel his eyes glazing over, and he scrunched them tight and opened them again to snap himself into alertness. Dirt and birdshit on the windshield. Eight eyes staring at gray-white blobs of hardened shit and slime.

We never have conversations anymore, I said.

Yes we do.

No we don't.

He tried to think of something to say. You got anything goin' on right now?

Ain't been laid in forever, I said. Back in opwaga again. In the back seat Phoebe rolled her eyes.

What's opwaga, Tobey said.

You know.

No.

Organization of people who aren't getting any.

We went down the hill. We curved around past the Cromwell Bridge exit. Do they call it Cromwell Bridge because of Oliver Cromwell? Adam asked. There's a conversation, he was thinking. Now I'm helping out and we're having conversations, he was thinking.

No, they call it that because there was a bridge there named Cromwell Bridge.

Tobey sped on around the curves. Cops are here with radar sometimes, he was thinking. He kept his sight focused on the shoulders, watching for stopped cars. His tires were skidding on the turns, and he was always conscious of the loose slippery feel of the wheel. The car was getting old. He thought about the rattling and looked in his rearview mirror and wondered why they weren't catching up.

Are we gonna run out of gas?

Shrug.

Tobey squirmed around in his seat. Coffee marks stained his jeans legs from knee to waist. Brown streaks of bile and booze the brown and remainders of coffee marks that stained his jeans; he hacked loudly the trailing smoker's cough that drumbanged our ears. His eye met the eye of a snowflake splinter in the glass of the windshield, locked, front and away and sandy stringy hair brushing against his collar-brushing shoulders. Two weeks' beard growth falling from his face; bird-blue eyes; chapped lips whose sheathes of dead skin vibrated against each other at the sound of oncoming car horns. How long for you now? I asked him.

Three months.

Quitter.

Huh?

Like it says on the sign at Crackpot. Right by the back counter where you ask them for cases from the fridge. He swerved back and forth within the middle lane as he massaged his hands against the wheel. Rehab is for quitters.

Tobey stared out the window. We passed Perring Parkway. South and north.

Isn't it.

Three months.

Surprised they don't care that you're drinking.

They do.

Mmm.

The speakers hummed. Click croak creak. Swiftly around the circle. What is the word, Tobey was thinking. Circumscription. Circumnavigation. Stringy sandy hair dangling in his face blocking his view: he tossed it back to the side. Whatever. He was tired. In the mirror he saw the redness of his eyes. Where the hell are they. In the mirror he saw what seemed to be a box-shaped shadow at the far bend of the road behind him; as we rounded a bend it disappeared.

How's Angeline doing? I asked him.

Angela.

Well?

I don't know.

The violence of his scoliotic shrug carried spite and scorn. Tension vectors untangled like a snapping coiled skein. Oh that's right she left.

How's your mom doing?

She's all right.

Coming down this weekend.

He nodded. Curling up his nose. Coiling up his nostrils.

I could see it. Just want a bump, man, he was thinking. Single fuckin' bump. With spittle swishing in his throat he tapped his wart finger on the wheel. White Marsh. Belair Road. How far now. All I wanted. He kept time with the rhythm of the music, sliding his middle finger up and down the plastic, imagining the murky tablature. Where are they. We're winning. Die in the attempt if. In lockjawed teeth-gritted clarity he saw the bloody bodies crashing into shivery bay brine, the barricades of the bridge soaring clunk into the water. Concrete will sink. D'you do you know this?

Change the song, Phoebe said from the back. Put it on the radio.

Tobey looked to the right. Do it you die.

I don't like this tape either, I said.

It's the Stones.

But I don't like it.

What are you trying to tell me?

I'm telling you that I don't like it.

That's fine. But I'm not going to change it.

Every time I go down the street. Some grandmomma start breakin' down on me. Stop breakin' down.

The road was nearly empty. We had the left lane to ourselves. We shot past the walls and trees and I-95 and cars streaked backwards in strong and straight trajectories into the rearview. Tobey kept the speed between a hundred and a hundred five. Still no sign of them. He looked at his hair in the mirror and adjusted a curl and tossed beer solemnly down his dry throbbing throat.

Past I-95 through Dundalk. Everyone was sleepy. Tobey rewound the tape back to the beginning of the song again. It was the fourth time through the song. He could feel Adam's agitation. The nerves running down his spine. Tobey listened to the words and waited again for the moment. The twelve or thirteen notes in perfect succession. Seven seconds of melody. The only part of the song he wanted to hear. Otherwise he wouldn't have repeated it. Wait for the melody to come: fingerdrum on the wheel as the melody drills down into fingerbone. The nerves in his spine. Plucked like guitar strings. Here it comes again. He gripped the wheel for a curve to the right. Here it comes here it comes here it comes.

The tollbooth, Adam said.

Goddammit you made me miss it again, goddammit, you piece of shit.

The tollbooth at the bridge.

Goddammit I listened through that whole song to hear those few seconds you piece of shit and you picked that moment to talk.

We're going to have to stop at the tollbooth at the bridge.

Tobey hung his mouth open.

I guess no one thought of that, Adam said. They all stared forward. Tobey shook his head in disgust with curled nose and gritting teeth speeding on towards the bay and in the rearview mirror peripherally he saw Adam's smug smile. The curt smile of Adam in the back seat.

You knew about the tollbooth all along, Tobey said, didn't you? Huh?

You knew it was there.

We all knew it was there.

You remembered it was there.

Whatever.

They're going to catch up, Tobey said.

Adam shrugged.

We'll just speed through it, Tobey said. How would you like that? How does that make you feel? Sitting back there in your preppy turtleneck sweater rolling your eyes at me thinking, You can't drive, you're going to wreck, you're going to kill me. Worrying. Thinking the tollbooth, the tollbooth, when we get there it'll all be okay. Your little trump card. The chips you were hiding under the table.

Whatthefuckever.

Silence. Driving on. No lights outside. No one talked and we passed some boring shit out on the road and Tobey tapped his finger on the wheel and we didn't see them behind us and the tollbooth and what are we going to do about it and we looked for cops and nothing happened for a while and it was boring. There were about eight or nine minutes which probably didn't actually happen which probably in a very literal sense did not exist. Driving on. Silence.

I looked out at all the houses. I couldn't see them but I knew they were behind the wall behind the trees behind the shopping centers. Somebody dose me. I see you ha ha I see what you're up to. Why do you want me here. Give me the reasons. In your red eyes next to me the reasons where are they.

I need to piss, Tobey said.

Piss into a bottle and throw it out the window.

I can't do that while I'm driving.

Oh well, I said.

You know what they should have for cars? he said.

What.

Some kind of tube that comes up that you could piss into and it would just be a hole straight down to the road. It could just pull up from the floor and you piss into it and just let it snap back down into the floor when you're done.

That's disgusting, Phoebe said.

You'd never have to stop. You could just keep driving forever.

You'd have to get gas, I said.

But you'd never have to stop except for gas.

I guess.

I should design it, he said. I'll patent it. I'll make millions. Thousands maybe.

Whatever.

We were coming up to the tollbooth. One mile. Well, Tobey said, we'll do what we can while we can. He pushed the gas to the floor. Pedal to the metal, Adam. The car shook. To the left. To the right. He was stretching out the tension in his neck. He was thinking about sex. How it had been three months. How Phoebe always ignored him. He was thinking about sex. He was thinking about jerking off. He was thinking about how the white lines on the road looked short but someone had told him they were six feet long on the interstates. He was wondering whether anyone could know what he was thinking. He doesn't know I can see his thoughts but something makes him nervous.

The one woman at the Grind. Eyeing me and I could see the connection as she latched on drooling for me to signal. Long smooth raven hair big brown eyes looked like a Paris model.

What are we going to do, I had said. Now that you've hooked onto my mind. We've got this power now the two of us as one. What are we going to do.

Her mouth hung open for a second before she turned and rushed out onto the street. She didn't understand I thought it was just a mistake I'd made but she understood. It scared her. They don't want me to know.

I can see these things. It's why I'm not scared in the car. Nothing will happen. Alone on a mountain at the age of eighty-seven heart failure painless plink into nothing. Until then nothing.

Nothing will happen until then.

Where do you think they are? I said. Vince and them.

He didn't answer.

Are you listening to me? I said.

What?

You don't listen to me.

Well what did you say?

You're not listening to me.

He'd been trying to hide it for so long but I found beneath his disguise the cold words the deadly hemlock raw concoction see glowglowing in our lofting little airboxpocket speeding toward the bay: gloat smirk many many layers but beneath it all of course the old riff. Can't do a damn thing without you tagging along. Staring. Hate it when you look at me, he was thinking. Your one beastly eyebrow, connected to itself. You think you know me. You think you're clever.

I think old Sudsucker whatever his name might have been saw the lonely purple aura. Above my head as I ordered the drinks. So he laughed.

I think this is very fast; it's a high bridge. The cold air hangs in frigid pockets waiting frail and bald hanging in heterogeneous suspension. I think it's almost three. Waiting outside in the spaces between thrusting air pockets looms the salt and the stench of the bay: I think I can smell it twisting off my nostrils. I think they'll catch up now. I think this is silly. I think therefore I am. I think I'm going to do something drastic. We're going to go swimming, I think.

Shit, he said, there's a line.

He screeched to a halt. There were five cars in front of us, and it took almost a minute for us to get to the front. Headlights approached slowly behind us. The car in front of us had to wait for a receipt. Tobey put his head down against the wheel as Vince pulled up behind us. I saw their smug smiles through the side mirror.

Goddammit, Tobey said.

We paid the toll and took off. The car sputtered forward. Behind us Vince didn't even stop at the tollbooth; he tossed the change at the attendant and followed us, never leaving our bumper.

Goddamn fucking piece of shit, Tobey said as he shifted from second to third. Fucking goddamn piece of shit.

In the mirror the roundness of my eyes and the circle in my skull plate swirling round again in circles. I like it when it looks this way. The whites of my eyes coated by a shiny film of liquid and look at all the white things: the whitecaps in the water and the lines on the road and Adam's knuckles wet with spit from where he has bitten them raw and the stars and the moon and the headlights behind us closer closer. Tobey revved it up to the line and shifted to fourth. You can't do it, man.

Goddamn fucking piece of shit, he repeated all the way across the bridge.

Without the left headlight their car did not shine in the light as they pulled out to speed around us. They jolted into fifth. Adam was smiling and I felt his smile drilling into the back of my neck the vindictive little sonofabitch cocksucker. The wind from miles away hungry you'll be in it.

Goddamn fucking piece of shit.

Glowing the cold words smirking beneath the layered riffs of his mind. Trying to hide it for so long. Lofting pocket of box of air of bay speeding toward the sea. He saw me staring. Hate it when you look at me, he was thinking. I sent a thought and he ignored me. Thinking only about the chase. About Vince. They're all thinking about Vince. Phoebe is thinking about Vince.

Goddamn piece of shit bitchass goddamn lump of a car.

You want to win, don't you.

I grabbed the wheel with my left hand. They were passing us. I pushed the wheel left and Tobey panicked and grabbed my hand pushing it away looking into my eyes all googly-goggly. For a second I couldn't tell anymore what he was thinking. Or maybe he wasn't thinking anything. Vince swerved all the way over to keep from smashing into us.

All the way to the left edge of the bridge.

Tobey stabilized us and shot us forward toward the end. All the drums on the radio blasting. All the eyes staring straight ahead at eight straight paths of apparition. All the gulls of the bay winding down through the air whining at us all googly-eyed glimmering hotwired shitting into the water in glee.

Fifth gear.

We zoomed over the bridge joints as their headlights wavered in the mirror and the tooting horn zoomed in angry cosine waves through the outer sphere of air.

What the fuck, man.
I shrugged.
What the fuck.
They were winning.
What?
They would have won.
He stared at me.
I thought you didn't want them to win.
He stared at me.
They knew about the tollbooth. Like you said. It was their strategy, I said. This was our strategy. We won.
Jesus Christ, man, it was just a game.
You wanted to win.
I didn't wanna fuckin' die, bitch.
You were trying to win, I said. Adam was watching us intently. Phoebe was rolling her eyes.
It was just something to do after the bar so we could keep drinking. Something to do so we wouldn't have to go home.
You wanted to win.
Vince is gonna kick your ass. As soon as we stop the car he's gonna come lunging out his door towards the car and I'm just gonna point toward you and shake my head and watch it all happen. He slowed down.
You wanted to win, I said.
He drove on around the circle. Back to exit two. Ritchie Highway. The gas stations the strip malls the sprawl. Vince is gonna kick your ass, he said. I looked into his eyes. There was a moment of doubt but then I knew it. Of course I'm right cause if I weren't then he wouldn't be saying this. I saw the cold and glowing words smirking from the cracks in his skull. I sent a thought:
I knew it would be okay. I knew nothing would happen.
But he wasn't listening. Just watching the lines of the road whizzing by and silence in his mind not listening to me or anything but the lines. Eighty-seven. The mountain. Nothing will happen. Listen to me as I make it not happen.

A Profile by Wyn Cooper

When asked about the role of martial arts in his life, Madison Smartt Bell replies that it gave him the opportunity to be bad at something. To those of us who have followed his career as a writer, it's something of a relief to know that this might actually be true. In sixteen years he has published nine novels and two collections of stories to almost universal praise, in addition to writing essays and reviews for *Harper's, The New York Times Book Review, The Village Voice,* and many other publications. He has taught at the Iowa Writers' Workshop, the 92nd Street Y, the Johns Hopkins Writing Seminars, and Goucher College, and his students have included Carolyn Chute and Darcey Steinke. In addition to writing numerous screenplays from his own novels and those of others, he is also an accomplished musician and songwriter.

Madison Bell was born in 1957 and raised on the family farm outside Nashville. His parents had gone to Vanderbilt and had been friends with Allen Tate and some of the other Fugitive poets. Bell's mother taught him how to read when he was four, and he began having an image of himself as an author "when I was not as tall as the table." "By the time I was seven," he says, "I thought the writer was the most powerful person in the universe—that's what I wanted to be." He went to a grade school that encouraged creative writing, and a high school that didn't. Near the end of his senior year, he had a spontaneously collapsed lung and was offered the choice of surgery or staying in bed for a couple of weeks to see if the lung would mend on its own, which it did. "Out of ennui," he says with a laugh, "I wrote my first real short story."

In need of a change, Bell applied to Princeton, which, to his great surprise, accepted him with a hefty scholarship. They had a creative writing program for undergraduates, rare in the 1970's, "but you had to show them a body of work to get in. I didn't understand the requirement was a paper tiger, so I left for a semester, moved back to Nashville, got a job, and wrote stories at night." He returned the next semester with an entire portfolio, "which was overkill, but I ended up in George Garrett's workshop and became one of the hundreds of people whose career he has started and fostered." In his four years at Princeton (described in hilarious detail in an early story, "The Structure and Meaning of Dormitory and Food Services"), Bell won four awards for his fiction and graduated summa cum laude.

After Princeton, Bell moved to New York, where he worked as a security guard, a production assistant, and a sound man for Radiotelevisione Italiana. The M.A. program at Hollins College (now Hollins University) in Roanoke, Virginia, followed. There, he studied with Richard Dillard and Rosanne Coggeshall, and continued writing some of the stories that would appear in his first collection. His classmates at Hollins included Jill McCorkle, Cathryn Hankla, and Kimberly Kafka. Bell also managed, in the intensive one-year program, to write his first published novel, *The Washington Square Ensemble,* which Viking put out in 1983.

After Hollins, Bell returned to New York, the locale for most of his early work. In "Zero db," the title story of Bell's first story collection, a sound man in a bar on 14th Street ends the story by advising, into his recording device, "Listen. Listen. Listen. We can never be too attentive to our world." The two novels that preceded the book of stories, *The Washington Square Ensemble* and *Waiting for the End of the World,* showed that Bell had already taken this advice. These two New York novels put a twenty-something Tennessean on the New York map. His characters represented everything about New York that scares (or used to scare) so many away: junkies, dealers, prostitutes, anarchists. At a time when *Bright Lights, Big City* was getting an abundance of attention, Bell was writing about a world that didn't come and go in a decade, a night world that told the rest of the story. His characters, he says, "are the guys that would have been mugging McInerney's characters as they stumbled out of the Odeon at three in the morning."

His fourth novel, *The Year of Silence,* took an unusual tack: it ends in chapter six, the only chapter from the main character Marian's point of view. The five chapters before, and the five after, are narrated by ten very different people who all knew—or thought they knew—Marian before her overdose. *Soldier's Joy,* published in 1989, was a long tour de force about a Vietnam vet who comes home to Tennessee and runs into his black childhood

Madison Smartt Bell

friend, a novel held together in part, as its titles implies, by blue-grass music. Bell's second collection of stories, *Barking Man,* appeared the next year, and the year after that saw the publication of *Doctor Sleep,* which Bell has described as "basically structured as a prayer." When he finished it, he realized "in a way I hadn't before that all the novels I had written up to that time were spiritual pilgrimages of one kind or another. Though they are by and large couched in the form of thrillers, they're essentially experiments in religion. My model for that is Dostoyevsky, who was basically a thriller writer with a lot of religious obsessions that he was trying to work out."

Doctor Sleep was Bell's eighth book in as many years, and it was the first time he took a break of longer than a week before starting his next book. Not that he wanted to rest, though: he felt that *Doctor Sleep* was the end of a trend in his work, and he wasn't sure where to go next. In his own view, his first novel presented "a rather complicated argument" between Islam and the Afro-Caribbean religion Santeria; his second had very much to do with Eastern Orthodox Christianity; his third, *Straight Cut,* which was more like a conventional thriller than the others, involved "philosophical Christianity under the aegis of Kierkegaard"; *The Year of*

Silence concerned life in a world without religion, based on the ideas of French existentialism; and *Soldier's Joy* went back to primitive Christianity. Bell's pilgrimage ended with *Doctor Sleep,* which embraced hermetic gnosticism and the writings of Giordano Bruno. "This seemed like the answer," Bell says. "I think the idea that the universe *is* divinity is viable as a fundamental precept for a reformed religion for our time."

While researching Santeria for his first novel, Bell ended up reading some books on voodoo, which fascinated him. While researching his second novel, he happened upon some studies of the Haitian revolution, and became especially interested in the character of Toussaint Louverture. Thus *All Souls' Rising* was born, a dozen years before its publication in 1995. Bell continued researching the only successful slave revolt in this or any hemisphere, and finally began writing the novel, very slowly at first, after the release of *Doctor Sleep.* He intensified his research, relearned French, and learned Creole—but there was one thing he could not do, because of an embargo: go to Haiti. The conditions under which he wrote the novel, he says, "were in a way ridiculous. I'd never been there, I didn't know any Haitians, and so I was relying entirely on historical records, which fortunately were pretty complete, and on anthropology."

The fact that *All Souls' Rising* was a finalist for both the National Book Award and the PEN/Faulkner Award, and that he was named one of *Granta* magazine's "Best American Novelists Under Forty," seems less important to Bell than the fact that "it was good enough to convince a lot of Haitians who've talked to me about it. For an outsider writing from the point of view of an insider, to get anybody on your side validated it." Bell knows a lot about the reaction in Haiti to his book, having made nine trips there in the four years since the book appeared. It has also done well in France, where he has read from it—in French. The novel is the first in a trilogy that will eventually cover the entire revolution, with Toussaint Louverture at the center.

Bell recently completed the second volume, *Master of the Crossroads,* which Pantheon will publish in the fall of 2000. "I tried to make this book less violent than the first one," he says. Indeed, the violence in *All Souls' Rising* got rather graphic. In *The New York Times Book Review,* John Vernon called it a "carefully drawn road map through hell." He also said the novel, "refreshingly ambitious and maximalist in its approach, takes enormous chances, and consequently will haunt readers long after plenty of flawless books have found their little slots on their narrow shelves." The only negative reviews seemed centered on the assumption that the violence was gratuitous. Bell received complaints from readers that the book gave them nightmares. "The real reply," he says, "is that it's supposed to."

The fact that Bell's maximalist approach has paid off critically is more than just a feather in his cap. In 1986, before he had turned thirty, Bell turned his sharp critical eye on the rising tide of minimalist fiction in an essay for *Harper's*, "Less Is Less: The Dwindling American Short Story." Taking aim at a few writers who Bell thought had far too much influence, his long, cogent essay sent shock waves across the literary landscape. Someone was daring to criticize the work of Raymond Carver and Ann Beattie? Was he out of his mind? Was Carver really guilty of "dime-store determinism," abusing his characters, "presenting them as utterly unconscious one moment and turning them into mouthpieces for his own notions the next"? Bell's argument was extremely convincing, though his courage took its toll. More than one person threatened to stamp out his career. "There was enough ire among powerful publishing types to do me harm, but obviously I'm still around."

Bell shares the position of writer-in-residence at Goucher College with his wife, the poet Elizabeth Spires. He has taught there since 1984, and has helped a small army of fiction writers find their way into print. He finds that teaching helps him immensely when it comes to editing his own work, because he stays in practice. What does he do in his spare time? He wrote a screenplay for Roger Corman about the San Francisco earthquake of 1989. Two current film projects, one based on *Doctor Sleep* and one on *Save Me, Joe Louis,* "are looking like they might happen." He is a first-rate guitarist, very partial to his Gibson Les Paul. A current book project involves that very instrument, as well as both a fictional and a real rock and roll band—and the songs of both.

Wyn Cooper attended Hollins College with Madison Smartt Bell. He is a poet and songwriter. His second collection, The Way Back, *will be published by White Pine Press in the spring of 2000.*

ABOUT ELIZABETH SPIRES

A Profile by A. V. Christie

Think of the word "spires" or the word "aspires," and you see ascendance, a reaching, a rising up, a breathing upon, a breathing into life—you hear the word "spirit." Elizabeth Spires's work seems deeply linked with all the facets and motives of these words associated with her name. Even in her first book of poems, *Globe,* published in 1981, one senses a poet of deeply metaphysical and transcendentalist leanings, its first poem "Tequila" already interested in "taking the only road / out of the valley, / the one that leads everywhere."

Born in 1952 in Lancaster, Ohio, Spires avidly read her way through the Children's Room of the Circleville Public Library. Her choices in books were particularly indiscriminate, "including about three hundred sappy biographies," she says. She then moved on to the *O. Henry Awards* volumes in another part of the library and remembers distinctly, when she was twelve, reading Flannery O'Connor's "Everything That Rises Must Converge." It was then that she decided she would be a writer. In retrospect Spires feels that probably one of the most defining gifts her parents gave her was the unspoken assumption "that girls could do anything that boys did... *and that they had a perfect right to.* I read any book that I wanted to, went to any movie that I wanted to, and had no curfew as a teenager. This in a fairly conservative small town where many parents were overprotective of their children." Though neither of Spires's parents went to college, it was assumed she would. She attended both parochial and public school, and although she never felt pushed, Spires pushed herself (she admits she was an overly serious child). Her decisions about going to the East for school, majoring in English, and becoming a writer met consistently with her parents' approval. "I guess they had faith that I would figure out some way to support myself as I pursued my goals," she says.

Although she thought she would write short stories, at Vassar College she started taking poetry workshops, studying first with

Jerry Bauer

Judith Kroll, then with William Gifford (he continues to be a crucial friend and discerning voice). She decided that if, five years out of Vassar, she had not had some "positive response" to her work, she would give up poetry altogether. Until that time, she would devote all her time and energy to it.

After she graduated, Spires worked in Columbus, Ohio, for an educational publisher as an editor and freelance writer of children's reading texts. Her poems began to appear in *The New Yorker, Poetry, The American Poetry Review,* and *The Partisan Review,* among other prestigious magazines. (Of course, this period was not without its sting: Spires recalls receiving, in a one-year span, fifty rejection slips in a row.) In 1977, Spires also approached Elizabeth Bishop, a longstanding influence, to ask for an interview; it was subsequently published in *The Paris Review,* and, as Bishop's last full-length interview, remains a vital literary record.

Spires moved to Baltimore in 1978 to pursue her M.A. at the Johns Hopkins University Writing Seminars. Her master's thesis eventually became the book *Globe,* described by Norman Dubie as "wonderfully born of metaphor...almost like a dream [these poems] reproach us, and still we wake refreshed."

Since that time Spires has followed with three more volumes of poems: *Swan's Island, Annonciade,* and *Worldling,* and several children's books—three published relatively recently. She's won grants from the Guggenheim and Whiting foundations, had poems appear in dozens of anthologies, and edited *The Instant of Knowing,* a collection of occasional prose pieces by Josephine Jacobsen.

Spires met her husband, Madison Smartt Bell, just as *Globe* was being published. She was giving a reading at a summer writers' conference in Maine where Bell was staff assistant to George Garrett. They were married in 1985 at the Ladew Topiary Gardens just outside Baltimore, and, except for a year here or there in London or Iowa, they have continued to live in Baltimore, both teaching at Goucher College, writing, and raising their eight-year-old daughter, Celia.

And now here Spires is at mid-career, a time she's looked closely at in other poets, such as Robert Lowell and John Berryman, for what can be learned from their shifts of approach. "I don't think it's some sort of phoenix-like redefinition for me," she says, "so much as a new stage or chapter that grows out of whatever was there before; there's no part of a life that springs out of nothing. I am still just writing poems about what is directly in front of me that's all-engrossing, trying to write really directly. I've never been prolific; for me poems are like major events. Even if they're about something small—that something may seem small to other people, but it doesn't feel small to me."

At middle age, she's realizing more than ever how important relationships are to parents, mentors, close friends—"those who have died, are dying, or are going to die"—and what's received from this older generation. "I don't think I realized. I thought middle age was about life, not death. If you're lucky, you're still far from your own death or halfway, but not all the way." Her poems now are exploring such losses and relationships, the ways one unwillingly advances into a void that is made up of loss, where, as she writes in a new poem, "soul to soul, / we would have forever / never to speak again."

"I see where the next book is heading; it is preoccupied with these losses," she says. "Middle age is about beginnings and ends. For me, at least. Especially if you become a parent in middle age." In her fourth book of poems, *Worldling* (Norton, 1995), Spires focused with a pressing intelligence on conception, pregnancy, and motherhood, on the exact ways in which these are transformative experiences. Her meditations on the subjects are immaculate and lyrical. In her poem "The First Day," she writes, "I have had a child. Now I must live with death."

"I know that that's a line that makes some readers cringe, but to me that's the way it was. You have to say it, but then you realize that the way you said it is probably not good enough. Maybe the line doesn't achieve it in language. I wasn't striving to be ultra-poetic. That line connects to what I'm still thinking about: my own mortality and the mortality of those close to me. And, too, there's the actual physical end: you start to wonder what happens after death, what shape and form are we in after we die? There's a subject for poetry!"

Spires says she's never thought in terms of giving herself formal writing projects. "When I was working on my second book, the one thing I thought about was that I had more of a sense of a line. I thought the syntax of my sentences was becoming more complicated and emphatic. I like writing poems with long lines the best, but I don't have ideas for them very often. You feel like you've got all the power in the universe behind you—you're in charge of the waves of the ocean: here I am making it all go and happen."

Some of the poems she's working on now are "shadowed by myths"—a poem, for example, about Robert Frost in which he compares himself and his wife, Elinor, to Cadmus and Harmonia. "These characters in myth are archetypal figures. Trying to see deeply into your life, you may, sooner or later, see it clearly in archetypal terms. There's nothing we can live through or experience that doesn't already exist as an archetype." Almost in one breath she has at the ready Philip Larkin's disparaging and snide corrective about poets' use of "the universal myth kitty." But, too, there is Allen Grossman's expansive and inspiring lecture on Orpheus, a piece she theorizes has resoundingly informed contemporary poets' uses of myth. Spires keeps "searching and scouring" for writing to excite her, for poets that she's not read at all. May Swenson and the Australian poet Gwen Harwood are her current amazements, just to name two.

A sense of her deepest writerly passions and resolve comes clear, though, as she discusses her writing for children. She is particularly taken with the phrase "a word-inspired world," used in one critic's review of her recent children's book *The Mouse of Amherst*. The mouse in question, Emmaline, becomes diligent wainscot apprentice to Emily Dickinson. Emmaline laments, "There was an emptiness in my life that nothing seemed to fill." Her longing to "touch something untouchable" leads her to poetry and to, as a *New York Times* critic notes, "the nourishing power of words." To Spires, this "word-inspired world," this world of reverie and imagination, is what completes one's existence, makes it feel full and whole. "Without it," she says, "the physical world seems impoverished. But with it, day-to-day life feels endless and infinite."

"Children who like to read, and who grow up with books in the house, easily enter the world I'm talking about," says Spires. "I'm concerned, though, at the number of children who don't know this world of words exists. The *way* a story or poem is written, as well as what it's about, can pull children into thinking about this whole business of language. It can make them think about the power of words and imagination and, possibly, how they can use that power themselves."

"For most adults, the relevance of poetry to their lives is even *less* than I would have believed it was in my twenties and thirties, and I didn't think then that I had any illusions. Most people appear to be living without poetry quite nicely. They may turn to poetry at some terribly critical moment—a birth or wedding or funeral. But how can anyone possibly commit to a life of words and not be concerned about what poetry has come to mean, what place it occupies in the present time and culture?" Her comments call to mind the fevered work of anthropologists trying to keep a foundering language alive. "You feel this force against you if you write serious fiction or poetry; you're trying to do your part. You hold on—blown horizontal—and just try to not let go of the tree."

Spires is thinking of a new poetry assignment for her students at Goucher College, based on May Swenson's poem "Too Big for Words." She'll ask her students to place themselves at that border between language and the ineffable, the very place from which Spires has so compellingly spoken throughout her career. Just as she says in her own introduction here, with "the edge of time so close," she continues to stand at each and every threshold resolutely, looks with directness as she is "lived by events." She attends to them, giving keen attention to everything from workmen raking seaweed into piles at the empty governor's mansion to how a white curtain on a fall afternoon can suggest the soul or time's continuum, its lifting a figure for the present's fluid move into the past.

A. V. Christie's first full-length interview with Elizabeth Spires appeared in 1995 in the Southwest Review. *She has since reviewed a number of Spires's books.*

IN THE SURGICAL THEATRE *Poems by Dana Levin. The American Poetry Review, $14.00 paper. Reviewed by Susan Conley.*

Dana Levin's first book of poetry, *In the Surgical Theatre,* resonates with the dual imagery of pain and healing, scalpel and angel. The poems move swiftly and seamlessly from the literal drama of the operating room—its stark lights and surgical knives—to the larger domestic theater of family abuse and emotional bloodletting. Winner of the inaugural APR/Honickman First Book Prize, selected by Louise Glück, this fiercely intelligent book is grounded firmly in the realm of American confessional poetry, but Levin wisely and skillfully manipulates conventional boundary lines.

The "future of the body" is in question here, and the rich symbolism of this corporeal and spiritual investigation supports this volume in a complex architecture. Lines between truth and fiction, history and autobiography, continuously blur in the book's dark, elliptical explorations, where we see "the limbless, the fractured, / civilians and factions / spilling out of its cornucopia of grief and divide" ("First Cradle").

"On February 9, 1965 I was slit through the belly / without anesthetic," the speaker of "The Baby on the Table" flatly declares. The poem then demands of the reader, "Have you ever been hurt, have you ever been cut, is it only / physical knives?" Earlier, in "Body of Magnesia," the speaker asserts unequivocally, "I was solid, I hurt, my wings could be broken, / it was joy, I was living in it, I bled, I cried." Clearly this collection is not for the squeamish or faint of heart. Levin's gaze is unflinching, and the reader is implicated and challenged at every turn.

In the collection's title poem, the disembodied speaker watches her father get cut down the middle and asks of the wound: "Do you want it to be stars, do you want it to be a hole to heaven, / clean and round?" The speaker then ascends to the realm of angels to watch the ensuing performance: "I came up here, to the scaffolding above / the surgical theatre / / to watch you decide. / Can you go on with this mortal vision?" What amazes in this collection is how various speakers hover over bloody bodies, over wreckage of nuclear families and inconsolable anger, and still choose to go back into the body because they "can't bear not feeling" ("Door").

A patriarchal father figure storms in and out of poems like a tornado: "And then we were in the cellar, / in the darkness with the jam jars, while he roared and tore past our doors" ("Wind"). The speaker is so disgusted with her father, "his sagging face of an idiot / struck dumb by grief," that she won't talk to him. Just when these themes of domestic revenge and hate feel too familiar, Levin broadens the agenda to include transgressions of a global scale: "the medics, the nurses, the mothers and fathers, generals and presidents, / hovering above the stink of ripeness and death" ("Personal History").

Levin's syntactical innovations are impressive: the lines sprawl and roam over the page, and then become tight and internal, almost as a defiance to convention. Enjambment speeds the poems up and helps in the difficult task of weaving the vast surgical metaphor from stanza to stanza. Yet, it is often the device of the angels that holds these disjunctive, wildly disparate poems together. Much is asked of these harbingers of life. Angels instead of surgeons handle the scalpels in the title poem, presiding over the sick, "perched quietly / on the rib cage . . . on either side of the hole like handles / round a grail . . ." They work furiously behind the curtain to "cocoon you, / to give you a stage . . ." Like Rilke's angels in the *Duino Elegies,* Levin's angels know pain and despair, but ultimately they are transcendent witnesses who give this fine book its wings.

HOW ALIENS THINK *Stories by Judith Grossman. The Johns Hopkins University Press, $22.50 cloth. Reviewed by Fred Leebron.*

In her first story collection, Judith Grossman, author of the acclaimed 1988 novel *Her Own Terms,* is boldly and decisively all over the map. *How Aliens Think* consists of lively and intelligent stories that are sometimes metafictional, sometimes realistic, sometimes philosophical, and always entertaining. Grossman appears, from the evidence of this collection, to be both a writer who can write any kind of story and a thinker who can infuse any situation with intelligence and a compelling blend of distance and compassion.

"Rovera" is a wonderfully controlled and precise story about a new mother watching—as if through glass—the slow death of her tubercular husband, an affliction that could have been prevented. Despite her anger and resentment, and her increasing detachment from her husband, she cannot fail to see "that every breath he drew in frightened him, as if something might tear open inside.... *If he were a dog,* the thought flitted through Vera's mind, alone in the kitchen boiling up milk, *we'd have to be thinking about putting him down.*"

The two central stories, "Spion Kop" and "How Aliens Think," follow a young Englishwoman who first sleeps with her married lover's brother and then immigrates to the United States in the hope of cementing a doomed relationship. These two fictions are clear-eyed and unsentimental, as "bad Susan" seeks a slice of peace and contentment in worlds from which she is clearly separate. The standing-room-only section of a Manchester United soccer game is a "vast, embittered, raging howl, with its feral descant of screams at the umpire...a slackening barrage of support and abuse." Manhattan "is one continuing assault of explosive noise and motion—insane jackhammers going at you from this side, backhoes clawing and grinding in the lot across the street, sirens in perpetual spasm." "There are aliens and non-aliens," she knows, and ironically consoles herself that even Hawthorne was "so obviously not on to himself." Ultimately, Susan is "like her fellow professional aliens": "there's no one to count on understanding how it felt, floating absently across the world while empires foundered under them."

In other stories, Grossman is more playful. "De Maupassant's Lunch: An Education" traces the possible trajectory in which a disembodied hand once owned by the poet Swinburne falls into the French writer's possession. "A Wave of the Hand" posits the idea that it is possible to grow up in a household where the father is a woman dressed in man's clothes, without anybody bothering to discuss or remark upon this fact. And in "From the Old World: Four Lives from a Saga," ancillary uncles and aunts occupy center stage in an ironic and brief family epic about the everyday and the odd. Throughout, the language finds new ways to invent the old,

as in this passing-on of one of the aunts: "And at some impercep-
tible moment in the next few hours, the kind Madge became as
old as she would ever be."

How Aliens Think is an eclectic and electric collection, in which
every page carries both a shock of recognition and a jolt of some-
thing tantalizingly original and new. "It's only to revise and set the
record a little straighter," the narrator in "Death of the Mother"
notes, immediately prior to the parenthetical close: "(Narrator
strikes fist over the heart)."

Fred Leebron is author of the novel Out West *and co-editor of* Postmodern
American Fiction: A Norton Anthology. *Knopf will publish his new novel,*
Six Figures, *in March 2000. He teaches at Gettysburg College.*

WHIRLING ROUND THE SUN *Poems by Suzanne Noguere. Midmarch
Arts Press, $12.00 paper. Reviewed by H. L. Hix.*

The title poem of Suzanne Noguere's *Whirling Round the Sun*
transforms a bus ride through a city in autumn into an epiphany,
in which "leaf / by leaf turning" serves as "a clue / to earth's revolu-
tion." The poem functions as the axis of the collection, and the
sense of awe that suffuses the part—"Sometimes it seems almost
beyond belief / to be here whirling round the sun"—pervades the
whole. Noguere sees everything as revelation, not for Augustine's
reason but for George Oppen's: the mundane conveys the mundus
because "Every object includes the universe in its constitution and
the laws of its being."

The first section in *Whirling Round the Sun* announces Noguere's
ambitions. Ours may be, as Baudrillard suggests, a culture of sur-
face, but that makes Noguere a dissident, insisting defiantly on
depth. The first lines of the book's first poem, "Ear Training for Po-
ets," set the tone: "As the owl in darkness zeroes in / on the world's
small sounds, so must you. But which? / The deepest comes from
any quiet room / where you can lie down undisturbed. So wait / and
listen." Drawing on a depth equal parts introspection and percep-
tual acuity, Noguere's nuance yields subtle but breathtaking results.
"THESCRIBESPACKEDCAPITALSACROSSTHEPAGE / as if they
were still chiseling stone until / at last in minuscules they fixed a
wedge / of space between the words and a hush fell / upon the page
as if light filtered through / trees to a forest floor." Nearly every page
recreates for Noguere's reader that forest-floor hush.

The second section's alnage of family history observes, in her ancestors' sewing and weaving, the unifying force in their sharing of modest domestic work. Noguere describes "Sewing with my Great-Aunt," and talks of the "Extremities" of one of her ancestors: "The doctor calls it *ulnar drift,* the way / your fingers now curve outward on both hands, / the bones driven like snow." She describes "My Grandmother Nellie Braun," who suffered a girlhood fall that left her stooped as short as "her last grandchild at ten," as possessing a spiritual stature far larger than her physical stature: "where she sat was center on each inner map, / with her hands folded in her quiet lap."

In poems about the hands and the brain, and the mysteries of their connection, the third section explores "how the body holds fast to pleasure." That exploration leads inevitably to a series of love poems in the fourth section, irresistible for its range and inventiveness. Some poems use Donne-like conceits, as when Noguere compares her beloved to a saguaro cactus in "Botanical Sketch of You" or compares the lovers to South America and Africa in "Continents": "one hundred / million years do not erode the fit." Another sounds like Hopkins's sprung rhythm: "We Who In / love's circus do love's fireball feat: eat / the witching flames; and lit by our own spotlight eyes vie / who is the better bareback rider." Yet another uses two haiku to woo the lover, "my hermit crab," home to "my lower lips" that mimic "the rose rim of / the pink-mouthed murex."

The final section foregrounds the natural world through which all the preceding poems moved. Its cornerstone poem about the American elm is as majestic as its subject, but the last poem (a final example of the masterful sonnets sprinkled liberally through the book) completes the whole collection by returning to the maples that appear in the book's first, middle, and last poems. Reiterating the fundamental themes of nature and mortality, the speaker wonders whether "the universe might fall / back upon itself" as the astronomers and the maple leaves seem to agree, or whether "the stars must fly / in one direction only like my life."

In the title poem, "the sparks / fly to my brain with their electric sign / for scarlet, then make my mind a mirror / of amber; and the effort is not mine," but the book, in contrast, represents tireless effort on the author's part. Each poem seems a moment's thought because the book embodies well over twenty years of stitching and unstitching. The polish of the poems in *Whirling Round the Sun* follows from the fastidiousness its author shares with predecessors like Larkin, Bishop, and Bogan, those who embody Rilke's ideal of "not reckoning and counting, but ripening like the tree which does not force its sap." No elm or maple offers better shade.

H. L. Hix's translation of Eugenijus Ališanka's City of Ash *will be published by Northwestern University Press in 2000. Among his other books are a poetry collection,* Perfect Hell, *and a book of criticism,* Understanding W. S. Merwin.

THE TRULY NEEDY AND OTHER STORIES *Stories by Lucy Honig. Univ. of Pittsburgh Press, $22.50 cloth. Reviewed by Pedro Ponce.*

The title of Lucy Honig's debut collection, winner of the 1999 Drue Heinz Literature Prize, echoes the familiar plea of fundraisers and activists to forget selfish personal concerns and remember the less fortunate. But for Honig, helping the truly needy can sometimes be a losing battle with hunger, addiction, and less tangible obstacles.

Maria Perez, the protagonist of "English as a Second Language," has survived persecution in Guatemala—including the loss of her husband and two sons—and made a life in New York City for herself and her remaining children. While she has overcome poverty and violence, she has yet to overcome the well-meaning condescension of her adoptive country. At a ceremony honoring her accomplishments in an ESL class, the mayor of New York turns Maria's recollection of an assassination into a political joke for the television cameras, minimizing the brutality she remembers: "Two older sons were dragged through the dirt, chickens squawking in mad confusion, feathers flying. She heard more gunshots in the distance, screams, chickens squawking. She heard, she ran."

In "After," need is purely personal. The summer after her father's death, Ellen Frisch works at his roadside produce stand and wrestles with her unresolved anger toward him. In one of the book's most evocative scenes, Ellen escapes to the shelter of a motel pool: "She forgot air, she forgot the limits of her lungs, she forgot the limits of her skin, which now interjoined with water." But Ellen's escape is short-lived: "[H]er head surfaced, and she breathed in the hot air, gasping like a fish that did not want air, and this air in her lungs and on her shoulders and around her face seemed to pull her body and mind into separate parts again."

The title piece, one of four linked stories that form the second half of the book, concerns Rita, the executive director of a New York City community group for the poor. Honig is unsparing in her portrayal of the politics that can affect even a charitable organization. When Rita, a staunch believer in 1960's idealism, decides to reach out on her own to a homeless woman, she finds herself in over her head. Later, livid that the woman missed an appointment, Rita sees her hunched form outside and chases her down: " 'I had *soup* for you, DeeDee,' Rita cried, reaching out for Deirdre's shoulder. 'And mocha torte!' As soon as she made physical contact, Deirdre lurched away and stood up straight, suddenly very tall. The scarf fell away from her face. But it was a man's belligerent, raging face, not Deirdre at all."

Just who are the truly needy? Are they the poor and homeless that society pushes aside? Or are they those who, in helping the poor, only foster another form of self-interest? These questions inform Honig's provocative collection.

Pedro Ponce's fiction has appeared in Gargoyle *and is forthcoming in* Alaska Quarterly Review. *He has published book reviews in* Rain Taxi, Washington City Paper, *and* Legal Times.

*Books Recommended by
Our Advisory Editors*

*New Books by
Our Advisory Editors*

Madeline DeFrees recommends *The Tiger Iris,* poems by Joan Swift: "Of all the writers I know, Joan Swift is surely one of the best at transforming reverses into poems of astonishing beauty and strength. Her particular blend of memory, imagination, feeling, and intellect creates an alchemy that changes the base metal of experience into gold." (BOA)

Don Lee recommends *A Gesture Life,* a novel by Chang-rae Lee: "This novel—a magnificent follow-up to Lee's first book, *Native Speaker*—has received a fair amount of media attention already, but enough cannot be said about it. Lyrical, powerful, truly remarkable." (Riverhead)

Philip Levine recommends *Lifelines,* poems by Philip Booth: "*Lifelines* is an astonishingly mature work of poetry that represents a life's work of dedication. The poems trace an adult's experience in the world from boyhood to old age, largely in the world of New England, and pay tribute to the toughness and decency of ordinary folk, who in these delicately paced and richly imagined poems are revealed as the extraordinary people they are." (Viking)

Madeline DeFrees, *Double Dutch,* poems: A limited-edition chapbook of DeFrees's poems that has been published in honor of this esteemed writer's eightieth birthday. (Red Wing)

Jay Neugeboren, *Transforming Madness: New Lives for People Living with Mental Illness,* nonfiction: In 1997, novelist Neugeboren delivered a moving and important memoir, *Imagining Robert,* about his mentally ill brother. Now Neugeboren examines the mental health care system as a whole, giving us a comprehensive, dramatic, and richly textured survey of failures and successes. (Morrow)

Joyce Peseroff, *Mortal Education,* poems: Peseroff's third book of poems recalls the raw experience of mortality, met through the illness and death of a friend, the context of history, and the tensions and pleasures of family life. Carnegie Mellon has also reissued Peseroff's *The Hardness Scale* as part of its Classic Contemporary Series. In *Ploughshares,* Robert Pinsky described Peseroff as "a clear-sighted, good-humored poet" who "has written poems that have the virtues many of her contemporaries strive for: she attains at times an unpredictable, colloquial poetry that adapts the casual, protective comic sense of a generation's manners to the demands of art." (Carnegie Mellon)

Robert Pinsky, *Americans' Favorite Poems:* An anthology of poems that were nominated for the Favorite Poem Project, the centerpiece of Pinsky's Poet Laureateship. Americans from all walks of life were invited to recommend their favorite poems, and thousands have responded with impassioned personal letters, some of which are excerpted here alongside the poems. This anthology reveals the rich, diverse presence of poetry in American life. (Norton)

Jane Shore, *Happy Family,* poems: Shore's latest volume follows the arc of her life from childhood in a closely knit Jewish family in 1950's New Jersey to her marriage and parenthood. In humorous, earthy verse, she bridges together experiences in the lives of women in ways both magical and profound. (Picador)

Gary Soto, *A Natural Man,* poems: In his new collection, Soto—who this fall was presented with the Hispanic Heritage Award—gives stirring, authentic voice to Chicano life in the San Joaquin Valley, where he was born and raised. (Chronicle)

ZACHARIS AWARD *Ploughshares* and Emerson College are pleased to present Elizabeth Gilbert with the ninth annual John C. Zacharis First Book Award for her collection of stories, *Pilgrims* (Houghton Mifflin, 1997; Mariner, 1998). The $1,500 award—which is named after the college's former president—honors the best debut book by a *Ploughshares* writer, alternating annually between fiction and poetry. This year's judge was John Skoyles, who is a *Ploughshares* trustee and the chair of Emerson's writing department.

Elizabeth Gilbert was born in 1969 in Waterbury, Connecticut, and raised in Litchfield. Her father was a chemical engineer, her mother a nurse, and, in their spare time, they ran a small Christmas tree farm on their property. The family lived in the country with no neighbors, and they didn't own a TV or even a record player. Consequently, they all read a great deal, and Gilbert and her sister entertained themselves by writing little books and plays. "I took this writing to school and fell in with a geeky crowd of creative, overly emotional girls," Gilbert says. "We were all very dramatic. In fifth grade, I wrote, directed, and starred in a play called *Mona's Proof* about a girl who goes back in time, but nobody believes her. It was a musical. There was one song in this play entitled 'No One Believes Me, No One Cares,' which I wrote myself and sang to the tune of 'Fifteen Miles on the Erie Canal.' We put on the play for the whole school. It was a big success. After that, nothing could stop my ambitions."

Gilbert went to New York University, where she majored in international relations and took Russian classes, thinking she might someday join the Foreign Service, so she could travel. She knew she wanted to be a writer, but she resisted taking literature classes and writing workshops. "I never thought that the best place for me to find my voice would be in a room filled with twenty other people trying to find their voices. I was a big moralist about it, actually. I felt that if I was writing on my own, I didn't need a class, and if I wasn't writing on my own, I didn't deserve one." This philosophy extended to M.F.A. programs. "Instead of going to graduate school, I decided to embark on my own education, to travel and work wherever I could, and to set my own goals for producing stories. I didn't want to spend any time whatsoever on a campus. I couldn't think of anything worse. I wanted to go out into the world and meet every last person I could."

She moved to Philadelphia and worked in a greasy spoon diner. She'd save as much money as she could, then travel—driving cross-country, flying to Europe, Mexico, Africa. When her money ran out, she would return to the diner. During this time, she kept journals, which served as background notes for the stories in *Pilgrims*. The title story was bought by *Esquire* in 1993—her first acceptance. When the story was published, she sent a copy of the issue to the publisher of *Spin* magazine, whom she had met a few months before, and included a note: "You should give me a job." He did. She pitched the idea for an article about "buckle bunnies," groupies on the professional rodeo circuit, and she was sent to Texas for two weeks. For the next three years, she was a staff writer for *Spin*, given free rein to create—as Gilbert puts it—the "off-beat beat, traveling to strange American places and writing about strange American subcultures." She carried that beat to *GQ*, where she is now a writer-at-large. "It's a natural complement to writing fiction," she says.

The twelve stories in Gilbert's collection are marked by her facility for dialogue, her breadth of place and character, and her playful and forgiving vision of human nature. About the book, Gilbert says: "I was trying to run as wide a range as I could with stories about people of all ages, all backgrounds, all levels of life. I did not want to write a thinly veiled, autobiographical, memoirish book. I wanted to tell stories about other people besides myself, stories about the kind of people I love and feel for in this world. And the people I'm attracted to tend to be of a kind— tough, smart, resourceful people who have fallen on hard times but who continue to do their best. People like my mom's relatives in Minnesota—tough farmers who've been through it all. It's a kind of American identity I am really moved by. I think the people in *Pilgrims* are joined by their desire to move their lives in a different direction, to relocate their entire selves. Hence the title. They're all looking for love or satisfaction elsewhere. They've been beat up a little, but they still have a sense of humor. And they are still capable of great acts of kindness to one another. They're shaky, but solid."

Gilbert's first novel, *Stern Men*—which covers a century of territorial wars between lobster-fishing islands in Maine—will be published by Houghton Mifflin in the spring of 2000. Now living in New York State with her husband, Gilbert has started work on a nonfiction book, *The Last American Man,* about a hermit in North Carolina who dreams of saving America by bringing people, one at a time, into the woods with him.

VOLUNTEERS AND TRUSTEES We would like to thank our interns and volunteer readers, who are listed on the second page of the masthead, for their extraordinary efforts. Our thanks, too, to our trustees for their continuing support: Marillyn Zacharis, Jacqueline Liebergott, DeWitt Henry, Carol Houck Smith, Charles J. Beard, William H. Berman, Frank Bidart, S. James Coppersmith, Elaine Markson, James Alan McPherson, and John Skoyles.

SUBSCRIBERS Please note that on occasion we exchange mailing lists with other literary magazines and organizations. If you would like your name excluded from these exchanges, simply send us a letter stating so. Also, please inform us of any address changes with as much advance notice as possible. The post office usually will not forward third-class mail.

CONTRIBUTORS' NOTES

PENELOPE AUSTIN is a community arts activist, co-owner of Changeworks, a center for arts education, and founder/president of the Coalition of Independent Artists and Artisans in Williamsport, Pennsylvania. Her poems have appeared in the Philadelphia Poetry in Motion series, *The American Poetry Review, The Kenyon Review, The Missouri Review, The New Republic,* and elsewhere. Essays on her experience with cancer were recently published in *Prairie Schooner.*

ALIKI BARNSTONE's most recent book of poems, *Madly in Love,* was nominated for the Pulitzer Prize. She edited the anthologies *A Book of Women Poets from Antiquity to Now* (Schocken, 1992) and *Voices of Light: Spiritual and Visionary Poems by Women Around the World* (Shambhala, 1999). She teaches at the University of Nevada, Las Vegas.

BRUCE BEASLEY is the author of three collections of poems, mostly recently *The Creation,* winner of the 1993 Ohio State University Press/*Journal* Award, and *Summer Mystagogia,* winner of the 1996 Colorado Prize. He teaches at Western Washington University.

GEOFFREY BECKER is the author of a collection, *Dangerous Men,* which won the Drue Heinz Literature Prize, and a novel, *Bluestown.* He has also received the Nelson Algren Award, an NEA fellowship, and a Tara Fellowship from the Heekin Foundation. He teaches at Colgate University.

JOHN BENSKO's books of poetry include *Green Soldiers* (Yale) and *The Waterman's Children* (Massachusetts), as well as *The Iron City,* forthcoming soon from the University of Illinois Press. He teaches in the M.F.A. program at the University of Memphis.

DINAH BERLAND's poems have appeared in *The Antioch Review, The Iowa Review, New Letters,* and other publications. She received a 1997–98 fellowship in poetry from the California Arts Council and works as a book editor for Getty Trust Publications in Los Angeles. This is her fourth appearance in *Ploughshares.*

KATE BOROWSKE lives in St. Paul, Minnesota, and is a librarian at a small, private university. She holds an M.F.A. in painting from the University of Iowa.

A. V. CHRISTIE's first book of poems, *Nine Skies,* appeared in the National Poetry Series in 1996, selected by Sandra McPherson. Her poems have been published in *The Iowa Review, Poetry Northwest, The American Scholar,* and the *Southwest Review,* among other magazines. A recent NEA fellowship recipient, she was Visiting Poet at Bryn Mawr College last spring.

MICHAEL COLLIER's fourth book of poems, *The Ledge,* is forthcoming from Houghton Mifflin. He is the co-editor, with Stanley Plumly, of *The New Bread Loaf Anthology of Contemporary American Poetry* (New England, 1999).

CAROLYN COOKE lives in Point Arena, California. Her work has appeared in *The Paris Review, The Best American Short Stories,* and in two *O. Henry Awards* anthologies. *The Bostons,* her first collection of short stories, will be published by Houghton Mifflin in October 2000.

WYN COOPER's second collection of poems, *The Way Back,* will be published in the spring of 2000 by White Pine Press. Recent poems appear in *Denver Quarterly, Fence,* and several anthologies, including *Outsiders.* He wrote the profile of Madison Smartt Bell that appears in this issue. He lives in Vermont.

THEODORE DEPPE's most recent book is *The Wanderer King* (Alice James, 1996). His work appears in current issues of *The Southern Review, Prairie Schooner, Green Mountains Review, Gulf Coast, The Minnesota Review, The Nebraska Review, Poetry Northwest, New England Review,* and *The Pushcart Prize XXIV.* "Translations from the Irish" is inspired by poems of Cathal Ó Searcaigh.

TIMOTHY DONNELLY's poems have appeared or are forthcoming in *American Letters & Commentary, Denver Quarterly, The Paris Review, Verse,* and elsewhere. His manuscript *Accidental Species* was awarded Columbia University's 1999 David Craig Austin Prize. He is co-editor of poetry at *Boston Review* and a Ph.D. student in English at Princeton University.

WALT FOREMAN earned his M.A. from The Writing Seminars at Johns Hopkins University in 1995. He is currently pursuing an M.F.A. in screenwriting in the film school at the University of Southern California. He has a story forthcoming in *Ontario Review.*

CAROL FROST is the author of two chapbooks and six full-length collections of poems, including *Liar's Dice, Day of the Body, Chimera, Pure,* and *Venus and Don Juan,* the latter two published by TriQuarterly Books/Northwestern University Press. A volume of her new and selected poems, *Love and Scorn,* is due out from TriQuarterly Books in the spring of 2000.

GEORGE GARRETT is the author of thirty books, and the editor or co-editor of nineteen others. This past fall, he edited *The Yellow Shoe Poets* (Louisiana). He teaches at the University of Virginia.

FRANK X. GASPAR is the author of three collections of poetry. His latest, *A Field Guide to the Heavens,* won the 1999 Brittingham Prize for Poetry. New work appears in *The Kenyon Review, The Georgia Review, The Bellingham Review, The Gettysburg Review,* and others. His first novel, *Leaving Pico,* was published in the fall by Hardscrabble Books/University Press of New England, and won a Barnes & Noble Discover Award.

BRIAN GLASER works as an English teacher in California and Mexico. He has studied poetry under Charles Altieri and Anne Middleton. "The World I Painted Twenty Years Ago" is his first poem to appear in print.

GREG GLAZNER's books are *From the Iron Chair,* which won the Walt Whitman Award, and *Singularity,* both published by W.W. Norton. His poems have appeared in *New England Review, Southern Poetry Review,* and *Third Coast.* He directs the creative writing program at the College of Santa Fe, where he co-edits *Countermeasures.*

LOREN GRAHAM is a graduate of the M.F.A. program at the University of Virginia and is currently a member of the creative writing faculty at Hollins University. His first book, *Mose,* was published in 1994 by Wesleyan University Press. "The Banquet" is part of a narrative sequence of sonnets in progress.

LAURIE GREER's work has appeared in *Poetry, The Virginia Quarterly Review,* and other literary journals. She won an Academy of American Poets Award in 1994. "Orpheus Crossing" is part of a longer sequence on modern and mythic violence. She lives in Washington, D.C.

ALLEN GROSSMAN is Andrew W. Mellon Professor of Humanities at Johns Hopkins University. His most recent books are *The Ether Dome* and *The Philosopher's Window,* both from New Directions, and *The Long School Room: Essays,* from Michigan University Press.

JEFFREY HARRISON is the author of *The Singing Underneath* (1988) and *Signs of Arrival* (1996). His poems have appeared in *The New Yorker, The New Republic, The Nation, Poetry,* and in many other magazines. He won a Pushcart Prize in 1998 and is a Guggenheim fellow this year.

WILLIAM HEYEN is Professor of English and Poet in Residence at SUNY Brockport. His books include *Erika: Poems of the Holocaust, Ribbons: The Gulf War,* and *The Host: Selected Poems,* from Time Being Books, *Crazy Horse in Stillness,* winner of 1997's Small Press Book Award for Poetry, and *Pig Notes & Dumb Music: Prose on Poetry,* from BOA Editions.

MARY-BETH HUGHES lives in Brooklyn, New York. Her fiction has appeared in *The Georgia Review.* She is a staff member of the Writing Seminars at Bennington College, where she has also taught fiction writing in the July Program. She is at work on a novel.

CYNTHIA HUNTINGTON's prose memoir, *The Salt House,* was published in August 1999 by the University Press of New England. Her most recent book of poetry, *We Have Gone to the Beach,* won the Jane Kenyon Award from the New Hampshire Writers' Project. She lives in Hanover, New Hampshire, where she is Director of Creative Writing at Dartmouth College.

JONATHAN DAVID JACKSON is a poet, dancer, and choreographer. He is a Presidential Fellow in Dance at Philadelphia's Temple University and a Visiting Lecturer in Jazz Dance Studies at the University of Illinois at Urbana-Champaign.

JOSEPHINE JACOBSEN's most recent book of poems, *In the Crevice of Time: New and Collected Poems* (Johns Hopkins), was a finalist for the National Book Award in 1995. Her occasional prose, *The Instant of Knowing,* was published by Michigan in 1997. She lives in Baltimore and received the Robert Frost Medal from the Poetry Society of America in 1998.

BETHALEE JONES is a recent graduate of Goucher College, where she majored in English literature with an emphasis in creative writing. Previously, she had a story published in *The Potomac Review.* She is currently writing a novel.

CYNTHIA KADOHATA was born in Chicago and grew up in Arkansas and Chicago. She is the author of the novels *The Floating World* and *In the Heart of the Val-*

ley of Love. "Gray Girl" is part of a novel in progress called *The Four of Us.*

SAMARA KANEGIS has spent several years researching and working within various North American circuses. Her first play, *Two Trailers,* was recently produced in Baltimore, and she is currently at work on a collection of short stories reflecting circus life. She resides in Baltimore and the Pacific Northwest.

ERIKA KROUSE's work has recently appeared in *The Atlantic Monthly* and *Story.* She received her M.A. in English/Creative Writing from the University of Colorado. She is currently living in Boulder, Colorado, and working on her first book of short stories.

MAXINE KUMIN has published twelve books of poetry, most recently *Selected Poems 1960–1990* and *Connecting the Dots.* Winner of the Pulitzer Prize in 1973 and the Ruth Lilly Poetry Prize in 1999, she has just published a murder mystery: *Quit Monks or Die!* She and her husband live on a farm in New Hampshire.

DAVID LEHMAN's poem in this issue, "December 25," is from *The Daily Mirror: A Journal of Poetry,* which Scribner is publishing in January 2000. The book consists of one hundred fifty of the poems he wrote after embarking on the experiment of writing one a day.

PHILLIS LEVIN is the author of *Temples and Fields* and *The Afterimage.* Her poems have appeared in *The Best American Poetry 1998, The New Yorker, The New Republic, The Paris Review,* and *The Nation.* She has been the recipient of an Ingram Merrill grant and a Fulbright fellowship to Slovenia, and is The Amy Lowell Poetry Travelling Scholar for 1999–2000. Her third collection, *Mercury,* is forthcoming from Penguin Putnam in the spring of 2001.

KATHY MANGAN's first full-length collection of poems, *Above the Tree Line,* was published by Carnegie Mellon University Press in 1995. Her work has appeared in *The Gettysburg Review, The Southern Review, The Georgia Review, Shenandoah, The Pushcart Prize XV,* and the new anthology *Boomer Girls.* She teaches literature and writing at Western Maryland College.

CLEOPATRA MATHIS's most recent book is *Guardian,* published in 1996 by Sheep Meadow Press. She teaches creative writing at Dartmouth College.

JOHN MCMANUS spent his childhood in Blount County, Tennessee, and studied English and creative writing at Goucher College and at the University of Exeter in southwest England, graduating in May 1999. *Stop Breaking Down,* a collection of sixteen stories, will be published by Picador Press in July 2000. Soon thereafter, he will begin graduate studies at Hollins University. He currently lives in Baltimore.

JONATHAN MUSGROVE's poetry has appeared in several journals, most recently in *The New Criterion.* He is currently enrolled in the graduate writing program at Hollins University.

D. NURKSE's forthcoming work includes *Leaving Xaia* and *The Rules of Paradise,* both from Four Way Books, and poems in *The New Yorker* and *The Paris Review.* He received the 1998 Bess Hokin Prize from *Poetry,* and teaches privately and in the prison system.

SUE OWEN's third book of poetry, *My Doomsday Sampler,* was published in the fall by LSU Press. In 1998, she received the Governor's Arts Award for Professional Artist of the Year from the Louisiana State Arts Council. She teaches in the English department at LSU as Poet-in-Residence.

PATRICK PHILLIPS is a native of Georgia who now lives and works in New York City. His poems have appeared recently in *DoubleTake, New England Review,* and *The Gettysburg Review.* He is a founding member of the Poison Clan collective.

STANLEY PLUMLY's *Now That My Father Lies Down Beside Me: New and Selected Poems* will be published by the Ecco Press next year.

LIA PURPURA is the author of *The Brighter the Veil* (Orchisis, 1996) and a collection of translations from Polish, *Poems of Grzegorz Musial: Taste of Ash and Berliner Tagebuch* (Fairleigh Dickinson, 1998). Her collection of lyrical essays, *Increase,* won the 1999 AWP Award in Creative Nonfiction. She lives in Baltimore.

JOHN ROBINSON is the author of two novels, *January's Dream* and *Legends of the Lost.* He has finished a collection of stories, *Centipedes on Skates,* and is at work on a novel, *The Finite Passing of an Infinite Passion.* He lives in Portsmouth, New Hampshire.

JANE SHORE's new book of poems, *Happy Family,* is just out from Picador USA. Her second Lamont Prize–winning book, *The Minute Hand,* will be reprinted as part of Carnegie Mellon's Classic Contemporary Series this year. Her third book, *Music Minus One,* was a 1996 National Book Critics Circle Award nominee in poetry. A *Ploughshares* guest editor in 1977, 1984, and 1997, she is a professor at The George Washington University.

CHRISTINE STEWART received a Ruth Lilly fellowship in 1998. Her work has appeared in *Five Points* and *Poetry.* She is currently enrolled in the master's program in creative writing at Hollins University.

SUSAN STEWART teaches poetry at the University of Pennsylvania. Her most recent book of poems is *The Forest,* published by the University of Chicago Press.

VIRGIL SUAREZ's most recent collection of poems, *You Come Singing,* was published by Tia Chucha Press/Northwestern University. A limited-edition book, *Garabato Poems,* was also issued by Wings Press in San Antonio. *In the Republic of Longing,* a new collection, is due out in the spring of 2000 from Bilingual Review Press. He teaches at Florida State University in Tallahassee, where he lives with his family.

JENNIFER TSENG received an M.A. in Asian American Studies from UCLA and has been awarded fellowships from the Millay Colony for the Arts, the Syvenna Foundation, Cottages at Hedgebrook, the Helene Wurlitzer Foundation, and the MacDowell Colony. Her work is forthcoming in *Green Mountains Review, Crazyhorse, Amerasia Journal,* and *Hawaii Review.* She is currently in the fiction program at the University of Houston.

MICHAEL TYRELL's first manuscript of poems, *Invisible Station,* was a finalist for the 1999 Yale Series of Younger Poets. His poems are in current or forthcoming issues of *The Paris Review* and *The Western Humanities Review*. He has reviewed books of poetry, fiction, and criticism for *Boston Review* and *The Harvard Review*.

BELLE WARING's first collection of poems, *Refuge*, was cited by *Publishers Weekly* as a "Best Book" of 1990. Her latest book is *Dark Blonde* (Sarabande), and she is editor of *River Hope*, an anthology written and illustrated by her students at Children's National Medical Center, where she is Writer-in-Residence.

MICHAEL WATERS teaches at Salisbury State University in Maryland. Recent books include *Green Ash, Red Maple, Black Gum* (BOA, 1997) and *Bountiful* (Carnegie Mellon, 1992). Forthcoming are *New & Selected Poems* (BOA, 2000) and his new edition of A. Poulin, Jr.'s *Contemporary American Poetry* (Houghton Mifflin, 2000).

CHARLES HARPER WEBB is a rock singer turned psychotherapist and professor of English at CSU, Long Beach. His book *Reading the Water* (Northeastern) won the Morse Prize and the Kate Tufts Discovery Award, and helped him win a Whiting Writer's Award. His book *Liver* won the Felix Pollak Prize and was published by the University of Wisconsin Press in 1999.

MARK WUNDERLICH's first book of poems, *The Anchorage*, was published in 1999 by the University of Massachusetts Press. He was educated at the University of Wisconsin and Columbia University, and has received fellowships from the Fine Arts Work Center in Provincetown, Writers at Work, and Stanford University. His poems have appeared in *The Paris Review, Boston Review, The Yale Review, Poetry*, and numerous anthologies. He lives in San Francisco.

C. DALE YOUNG's poems recently appeared or are forthcoming in *The Paris Review, The Partisan Review, Salmagundi, The Southern Review, The Yale Review*, and elsewhere. He works as a physician at the UCSF–Stanford Medical Center in San Francisco and as Poetry Editor of *New England Review*.

ANDREW ZAWACKI is co-editor of *Verse* and writes reviews for the *TLS*. His poems have appeared in *Colorado Review, Denver Quarterly, Boston Review, The New Republic, Fence, Black Warrior Review, Agni, The Antioch Review, The Yale Review*, and elsewhere. He studies in the Committee on Social Thought at the University of Chicago.

∼

GUEST EDITOR POLICY *Ploughshares* is published three times a year: mixed issues of poetry and fiction in the Spring and Winter and a fiction issue in the Fall, with each guest-edited by a different writer of prominence, usually one whose early work was published in the journal. Guest editors are invited to solicit up to half of their issues, with the other half selected from unsolicited manuscripts screened for them by staff editors. This guest editor policy is designed to introduce readers to different literary circles and tastes, and to offer a fuller representation of the range and diversity of contemporary letters than would be possible with a single editorship. Yet, at the same time, we expect every issue to reflect our overall standards of literary excellence. We liken *Ploughshares* to a theater company: each issue might have a different guest editor and different writers—just as a play will have a different director, play-wright, and cast—but subscribers can count on a governing aesthetic, a consis-tency in literary values and quality, that is uniquely our own.

SUBMISSION POLICIES We welcome unsolicited manuscripts from August 1 to March 31 (postmark dates). All submissions sent from April to July are returned unread. In the past, guest editors often announced specific themes for issues, but we have revised our editorial policies and no longer restrict submissions to thematic topics. Submit your work at any time during our reading period; if a manuscript is not timely for one issue, it will be considered for another. We do not recommend trying to target specific guest editors. Our backlog is unpre-dictable, and staff editors ultimately have the responsibility of determining for which editor a work is most appropriate. Mail one prose piece and/or one to three poems at a time (mail genres separately). No e-mail submissions. Poems should be individually typed either single- or double-spaced on one side of the page. Prose should be typed double-spaced on one side and be no longer than twenty-five pages. Although we look primarily for short stories, we occasionally publish personal essays/memoirs. Novel excerpts are acceptable if self-con-tained. Unsolicited book reviews and criticism are not considered. Please do not send multiple submissions of the same genre, and do not send another manu-script until you hear about the first. *No more than a total of two submissions per reading period.* Additional submissions will be returned unread. Mail your man-uscript in a page-size manila envelope, your full name and address written on the outside. In general, address submissions to the "Fiction Editor," "Poetry Editor," or "Nonfiction Editor," not to the guest or staff editors by name, unless you have a legitimate association with them or have been previously published in the magazine. Unsolicited work sent directly to a guest editor's home or office will be ignored and discarded; guest editors are formally instructed not to read such work. All manuscripts and correspondence regarding submissions should be accompanied by a self-addressed, stamped envelope (S.A.S.E.) for a response; no replies will be given by e-mail or postcard. Expect three to five months for a decision. We now receive over a thousand manuscripts a month. Do not query us until five months have passed, and if you do, please write to us, including an S.A.S.E. and indicating the postmark date of submission, instead of calling or e-mailing. Simultaneous submissions are amenable as long as they are indicated as such and we are notified immediately upon acceptance elsewhere. We cannot accommodate revisions, changes of return address, or forgotten S.A.S.E.'s after the fact. We do not reprint previously published work. Translations are wel-come if permission has been granted. We cannot be responsible for delay, loss, or damage. Payment is upon publication: $25/printed page, $50 minimum per title, $250 maximum per author, with two copies of the issue and a one-year subscription.

Ploughshares Donors

With great gratitude, we would like to acknowledge the following
readers who generously made donations to *Ploughshares* during
our 1999 fundraising campaign.

Anonymous (33)
Sharon Anson
Leo Baefsky
Patricia Boudreaux
Vanita Brown
Scott Buck
Debra Crosby
Chadwick L. Dayton
Ronald De Luca
Paula Eder
Lynn Emanuel
Alice and Ken Erickson
David Ferry
Lee Gould
Ann Graham
Joy Harjo
Lucy Honig
Mabelle Hsueh
Irish Books & Media, Inc.
Gish Jen
Ruth M. Kelly
Maxine Kumin
David Lehman
Harold Lohr
Kay Maris
Alice Mattison
Kenneth Mintz
Mary Lambeth Moore
Patricia Polak
Georgiana Porton
Tim Seibles
Timothy Seldes
Tom Sleigh
James R. Sloane
Gary Soto
Maura Stanton
Candice Stover
Daniel Tobin
Mel Waggoner, First Choice Books
Gale Ward
Larry Williams

INDEX TO VOLUME XXV

Ploughshares · A Journal of New Writing · 1999

Northern Waters

JAN ZITA GROVER

"Grover clearly belongs in the same league with such outstanding contemporary nature writers as Annie Dillard, Kathleen Dean Moore, John Gierach, and Bill Barich. Fascinating reportage from a place where water, words, and nature converge." *Booklist* (starred)

$14.00, Paperback (1-55597-294-2)

The Delinquent Virgin

LAURA KALPAKIAN

The author of *Graced Land* brings us stories undaunted by the ordinary constrictions of time and place. *The Delinquent Virgin* shows us once again why the *Washington Post* calls Kalpakian's work "earthy, magical, compassionate, and inventive to the last detail."

$14.00, Paperback (1-55597-295-0)

Glyph

PERCIVAL EVERETT

"Percival Everett's infant genius protagonist vaults out of the playpen like Voltaire in flaming diapers—to dispatch Theory's charlatans, kidnappers and con men in this brilliantly, wildly parodic romp. Deconstruct THIS!!!" *Carol Muske-Dukes*

$22.95, Hardcover (1-55597-296-9)

Pastoral

CARL PHILLIPS

Carl Phillips's last book, *From the Devotions,* was named a Finalist for the National Book Award. This new title both enlarges and defines his already impressive literary territory.

$14.00, Paperback (1-55597-298-5) Available in January 2000

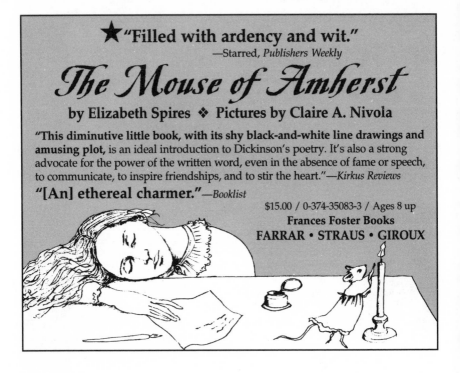

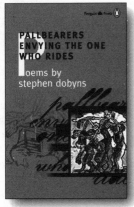